A JOHN CATT PUBLICATION

BEING THE CEO

The six dimensions of organisational leadership

MICHAEL PAIN

First published 2019

by John Catt Educational Ltd,
15 Riduna Park, Station Road,
Melton, Woodbridge IP12 1QT

Tel: +44 (0) 1394 389850
Fax: +44 (0) 1394 386893
Email: enquiries@johncatt.com
Website: www.johncatt.com

ISBN: 978 1 912 906 07 9

Set and designed by John Catt Educational Limited

This book is dedicated to the memory of James Eedy

Acknowledgements

I would like to thank the entire team at Forum Strategy for their exceptional work and for their support and advice in the writing of this book. For Sarah, Rachael and Lesley.

For Evelyn and Eliza.

About the author

Michael Pain is CEO of Forum Strategy. Under his leadership the organisation has moved from a start-up business to becoming a 'sector leader', supporting and advising hundreds of multi-academy trust (MAT) leaders nationwide through Forum's five regional CEO networks and beyond.

Michael's thinking and advice has been published in a range of education media, including articles in Schools Week, TES, Academy Today, and Education Executive. He has also led a number of high profile policy-roundtables with organisations such as Ofsted and the National Governance Association, including on the future of MAT accountability and the recruitment and training of trustees.

Michael speaks regularly on leadership, vision and responding to the contextual issues facing the education system and society, sustainable organisational improvement, and policy and research development. He also draws on his work advising CEOs, and his own experience as a successful entrepreneur, establishing a successful and highly respected national business with an excellent team of employees and associates alike.

Michael was formerly Head of Policy at the National College for School Leadership and, before that, an adviser to a number of politicians. He was called to the Bar in 2007.

Contents

Introduction

The job of CEO is almost impossible to define. It is the most powerful and influential position in any organisation, yet very little literature exists that attempts to provide a formula for doing the job, never mind doing it well. In many respects, that is to be expected. Every organisation is different, and every leader is different, and what works for one person in one context, may not work for another elsewhere. The role, and the reasons why people succeed or fail at it, remains, to a certain extent, an enigma.

It would seem to some that succeeding in the CEO role is as much about luck as it is about skill or judgment. There's certainly a degree of luck involved, but in reality much depends on a leader's ability to focus relentlessly on the right things ('the business they are in' and the areas where they have influence), on their contextual wisdom in response to the environment in which they find themselves, and their ability to accrue, mobilise and unleash resource (be it their people or investment) in line with that conceived wisdom. Success also undoubtedly depends on a CEO's ability to do all of the above, whilst providing ethical, values-based leadership.

What is possible is an attempt to provide some principles for those embarking on the CEO role. This book is intended to be like a clear night sky, guiding a CEO (or aspirant CEO) with reference to a series of major stars and constellations, rather than doing the impossible task of providing a detailed map for navigating the distinct mountains, forests and streams of a specific environment. This book will reflect on the mindsets, the nature of the relationships, and the approaches of those at the top of thriving organisations.

A CEO's work is rarely done, and as different contexts and circumstances provide unique challenges and approaches, so too do different moments in time. The role can evolve, and what applies to a new CEO or a CEO of a struggling organisation may not apply to the established CEO whose organisation is currently at the top of its game. As we shall see, even an established and, thus far, successful CEO can face potential pitfalls.

This book is written with a new breed of CEO in mind. In England, over a period of just six or seven years, we have seen the role of academy trust CEO proliferate as groups of schools working in collaboration have formalised their relationships and become 'trusts' – working under a single trust board and operating within the same legal entity. These organisations have developed shared senior leadership through their accounting officer (the CEO) and their central functions, bringing a whole new dimension to how schools and their closely related support functions – including school improvement services – are run. Some, mainly headteachers, have either stepped up to become CEO of these groups or, in some cases, taken a half-step to the role of 'Executive Headteacher'. This book is not about Executive Headteachers, as it is unlikely that this role will remain the one synonymous with the accounting officer role as these trusts grow in size and scale. It is impossible for someone to play a 'headteacher' role – executive or otherwise – across more than four or five schools, and it is certainly impossible at this level for them to balance the role of corporate leader with lead practitioner.

The transition from Executive headteacher (lead practitioner) to CEO (corporate leader) is far more challenging and perilous than some anticipated. It has been demonstrated time and again that being an accomplished headteacher or even Executive Headteacher is no guarantee of becoming a great CEO. There is a huge transition to be made. The leader must again become chief learner rather than the chief expert. Some have flourished as CEOs, whilst others, mainly through their inability to reinvent themselves as chief learners, have ended up a case study in how not to do it.

So where do we begin? This book will consider at its centre Forum Strategy's six dimensions of the CEO role, reflecting on examples from within and beyond the academy trust world. It will reference the policy environment trusts are operating in (the 'weather' as I like to call it). It will also consider examples of those CEOs who have made grave mistakes and those who have turned around generational failures within their organisations; and, it will also reflect upon the societal and economic challenges that will define the tenures of so many of this generation of CEOs.

In addition, it will draw on my conversations with many dozens of CEOs through our nationwide CEO leadership development networks, and apply my own experience of taking a start-up organisation to one with national reach as one of the academy trust sector's leading 'voices'.

Most of all, this is a book intended to help CEOs navigate their own path, based on their own values and the context they face, in the best interests of those they serve. After all, that is the ultimate role of all leaders.

Forum Strategy's **framework for the CEO role** to inform training, coaching & perfomance management

The six dimensions of the CEO role

- Translating vision into a leadership narrative
- Building an open, transparent & constructive relationship with the board
- Being the Chief Talent Officer & Culture Maker
- **Enabling** improvement and innovation as an 'organisational habit'
- Securing organisational sustainability and compliance
- Fostering key relationships, building social and professional capital

Leadership narrative

| **Clarity:** Knowing what business we are in | **Contextual wisdom:** Developing a deep connection with those you serve | **Legacy mindset:** Not letting 'short term' goals determine the long game | **Ethics & standards:** That which we will inevitably model to & encourage in others |

The four foundations of the CEO role

ForumStrategy

© Forum Education Limited 2018

11

Chapter 1

The four foundations of the CEO role

'What we realised is that the more we're true to ourselves, the better we are.'
– Jorgen Vig Knudstorp, CEO of Lego

What is the job of the Chief Executive Officer (CEO)? In its most functionary sense the CEO is the ultimate accountable officer of the organisation, the one who is the chief decision maker, the prominent puller of the levers of power and money. The CEO bestows the most senior positions, and is the one who can take them away; the person whose calls are always answered, by senior staff and by suppliers alike. The one who can divert resources and – to a degree – change strategy in an instant if they so wish.

Yet the CEO is not some omnipotent power. Indeed, any CEO who believes that their title or the resources and money that they can direct will guarantee success is misguided. This is certainly the case in 2019. In an era of sheer complexity, where the influence of technology is all pervading and where money (at least in the public sphere) is tight, the CEO must understand that power is more distributed and more unpredictable than ever before. In the knowledge economy, the saying 'knowledge is power' has never been more apt. CEOs must recognise that both the knowledge and the capacity to achieve change, improvement, and innovation is distributed at all levels within, and beyond, their organisations. It does not all – by a long shot – exist only within the CEO's office.

The CEO as farmer

The analogy of the farmer helps to better understand the role of the CEO. Like a farmer, the CEO does not choose the weather (either the policy environment or the economic context within which they operate) and they do not get to choose the quality of the soil (an organisation is limited – at least in the short to medium term – by the resources and capital at its disposal). The CEO must nurture that soil, feeding it, nourishing it, and cultivating it over time.

The farmer is also dependent on the market – the people who will buy the produce that they harvest each year, and whose appetites and tastes may fluctuate or wane. The CEO can rarely influence the fundamental needs and expectations of their end-users, they can only respond to them.

Ultimately, the farmer also cannot absolutely guarantee the successful development of the hundreds of thousands of seeds (the process of organisational growth and the quality of its output). However, what they can do is respond to a combination of factors (and more) through careful planning, relationship building, investment and a good dose of luck.

A CEO is – in essence – a farmer whose life, work and fate is influenced by the conditions. Responding to those conditions takes time and wisdom. When we look at it this way, the question 'what is the job of CEO?' becomes almost meaningless. Instead, it encourages us to ask not 'what is the role?' but 'where does the role have most influence and how can this be brought to bear to increase the chances of success to the highest possible degree?' The environment the CEO operates within determines much of that.

A CEO, like a generational farmer, is also subject to the limitations of guiding hands. The generational farmer is the custodian on behalf of a long generational line – for them, an invisible but ever-present force and source of accountability. This is instilled in the young farmer from an early age, and so it should be with the CEO from the outset of their tenure. The CEO is custodian on behalf of their governing board and all that it represents – the community, the ethos, the mission and values that define the organisation. To veer too far from these guiding hands (invisible or otherwise) would, in both cases, be unthinkable. Much like a farmer derives both support and accountability from a long-standing sense of responsibility and custodianship that transcends the generations, the CEO does so from a strong and ethical governing board of directors, trustees or partners.

So, it is within these limitations and ever-changing dynamics that a CEO must recognise and exert their power and influence with the most positive effect. The farmer, reading the weather, nurturing the soil, responding to the demands of the market, and understanding and respecting the limitations of their custodianship.

To respond to the environment, the CEO requires a firm base from which to lead and it is upon these four foundations that a CEO must embark and pursue the strategies that will define their tenure.

My four foundations of the CEO role are loosely based on a seminal article by A. G. Lafley, the former CEO of Procter and Gamble, which appeared in Harvard Business Review ten years ago.[1] Lafley, who has been described as one of the most lauded CEOs in history and credited for revitalising Procter and Gamble in the early 2000s, defined the platform of the CEO role as follows:

1. Defining and interpreting the context and how the organisation should respond.

2. Answering time and again the two-part question, 'what business are we in and what business are we not in?'

3. Balancing sufficient yield (or focus/results) in the present with necessary investment in the future.

4. Shaping the values and standards of the organisation.

---

1. Lafley, A, G. (2009) 'What Only the CEO Can Do'. (Harvard Business Review) Available at: https://hbr.org/2009/05/what-only-the-ceo-can-do

I have reflected on these as forming the basis of the four foundations for the CEO role, the firm footing as it were, upon which the CEO can proceed to shape both their leadership narrative and their strategy in order to take the organisation forward.

The following are the four foundations of the CEO role as I have defined them, based on this and other sources of research and thought leadership:

1. **Clarity of mission (or 'why'):** knowing what business we are in.

2. **Contextual wisdom:** developing a deep connection with, and understanding of, the context and those you serve.

3. **A legacy mindset:** not letting 'short-term' goals determine the long game.

4. **Ethics and standards:** that which you wish to model so that others become.

These foundations form the vision and values of the organisation at a given time. It is essential that they be firmly in place if the CEO is to proceed successfully in the role of translating vision into a leadership narrative and subsequent organisational strategy. On which note, I would also add a fifth, the 'gateway' foundation, which is the central tenet of this book, essentially.

5. **Understanding what the role of CEO is and what it is not:** the six dimensions of the role itself.

By considering foundations one, two and three together, we essentially create the vision for the organisation. As we will see later, unless the CEO is also the owner of the business (which is the case in some family businesses but not in public or charitable organisations), they do not set the vision. It is up to the board to establish the vision based on a clear discussion between themselves, key stakeholders – including staff and partners, and end-users; and, with reference to the CEO. The CEO's role in all of this is important in ensuring that crucial interplay is made between the context – 'the meaningful outside' (something they have so often unique organisational perspective of) and the mission – 'the business we are in'.

Three elements of a compelling vision

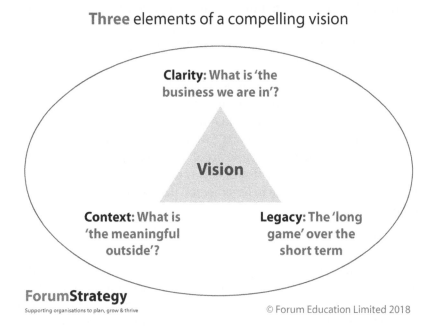

Clarity: What is 'the business we are in'?

Vision

Context: What is 'the meaningful outside'?

Legacy: The 'long game' over the short term

ForumStrategy
Supporting organisations to plan, grow & thrive

© Forum Education Limited 2018

However, the board, quite rightly, plays the most influential role in ensuring the four foundations are in place. The CEO must check that they are in place, and, if necessary, nudge their board towards cementing them. If the foundations do not exist, the aspirant or new CEO should consider walking away – as some do!

Let's take 'the business we are in' first of all.

Foundation one: Clarity and knowing 'what business you are in'

Lafley describes this as 'knowing what business you are in and knowing what business you are not in.' My view is that this is essentially the mission of the organisation. It is impossible for the board and the CEO to make sense of the dynamics within which their organisation operates and how they must respond to them if there is not a strong sense of the organisational mission to begin with.

Many readers will be familiar with Simon Sinek's work and the importance of having an organisational 'why'. The importance of having clarity about the business you are in – or as Sinek says, 'what gets you out of bed in the morning', is essential.

Indeed, having a clear focus as to what your organisation is seeking to achieve, and its overarching purpose is crucial in an increasingly complex world. The board and CEO must be rooted in this in order for them to make sense of the context they are operating in and how they should interact with it and influence it in order to work towards the desired outcome over time. However, it is possible for the organisation's sense of the business it is in to be either too narrow or specific or, indeed, too malleable.

Let's consider a 'why' or sense of mission that is too undefined or malleable. Business literature is littered with examples of organisations that diversified so much – losing sight of their 'why' – that they drifted by overreacting to the latest 'fads'. They lost all focus on the motivations and beliefs that attracted people to lead, work for them, and use or buy their services in the first place. Having too little sense of 'the business we are in' can soon see the organisation descend into being everything to everyone, yet nothing to anyone.

At the same time, a very narrow or too specific 'why' can stifle the ability to innovate or observe closely related trends. Such organisations' visions, as a result, do not sufficiently change or adapt with the times. 'The business we are in' must be allowed to 'interplay' with the context to a degree so that the organisation remains relevant and successful in a world of ever-changing forces and dynamics.

It is this careful 'interplay' between 'the business we are in' and contextual wisdom (together with the legacy mindset) that forges the organisation's vision. This, especially in today's fast-paced and ever evolving world, must be revisited regularly. The direction of the ship is generally pointed to the same destination, but the course must change from time to time in order to ride the currents and overcome the storms ahead.

This is something that is already evident in some multi-academy trusts. Being clear on what is meant by the destination, the 'why', is essential.

Take the multi-academy trusts that is so focused on 'scores on the doors' of test results and Ofsted grades (the key but very narrow focus of government targets). They miss the impact of the health and wellbeing of students on their ability to learn, and the preparedness of their pupils for a rapidly evolving jobs market.

The question of 'what business we are in' is one that needs careful thought and reflection. In this example, one could ask 'is it about getting pupils good test results?' (a very narrow focus, but one some academy trusts pursue above all else). Or 'is it about preparing pupils to live happy and successful lives? (a broader focus, which still needs careful thought as to how far an academy trust can have influence as it risks a diversification of focus that can exhaust an organisation). Being absolutely clear about 'what business we are in' defines the vision, and therefore the CEO's outlook, relationships, focus, decisions, and time. It is a key question that must be asked and agreed, with the board and others, before the CEO can go out into the world and perform that important interplay between the organisation and the dynamics that define its context and – ultimately – its work. Without being rooted, a CEO has no compass for navigating the role.

The 'business we are in' remaining too rigid: Blockbuster

The rapid rise of online film streaming services offered by the likes of LoveFilm, Amazon and Netflix made Blockbuster's video and DVD business model practically obsolete. The organisation was very much focused on 'the business it was in' – a high street home video rental service – right until the end.

What its board failed to do in setting the vision in the years leading up to 2013 was to create sufficient interplay with the second foundation, contextual wisdom. It failed to identify or respond to the changing expectations and behaviours of its customers. The emphasis that shifted towards ease of access (first through to delivery and then online streaming) and variety of choice. The vision was stagnant and provided no basis for creating a strategy that would succeed. The business model needed radical change, but Blockbuster failed to adapt its almost too strong, too well defined sense of the business it was in, in a way that kept up with the emerging and unavoidable contextual wisdom. The business collapsed as a result.

Losing sight of 'the business we are in': Lego

An example of a company that lost focus on 'the business it was in' was Lego. In 2003 Lego was on its knees. The organisation faced the biggest loses in its history – £217 million. The company seemed destined for bankruptcy.

The new CEO, Jørgen Vig Knudstorp, set out about engaging with and listening to the company's customers and staff. What he found was a company that had lost focus on the things that mattered to them: the business they considered themselves to be in. This was, above all else: the opportunity a toy gives a child to learn how to think systematically and creatively, whilst being easy to put together and hard to pull apart.

Instead of refining and adapting this core product and experience in a changing market, he found that the company had tried to diversify and take on new product-lines in a knee jerk response to developments such as the emergence of the video games market that grew in the '90s. It had become almost too focused on reading the context (foundation two) – but had failed to root this in the company's bread and butter – the reason people got out of bed in the morning to work for or buy Lego! 'What we realised is that the more we're true to ourselves, the better we are', says Knudstorp[2], quoting T. S. Eliot's 'Little Gidding': 'The end of all our exploring will be to arrive where we started and know the place for the first time.' The company had placed too much onus on responding to the contextual outside that it lost sight of 'the business we are in'; its sense of mission.

In response, Knudstorp sold off all parts of the business that weren't absolutely integral to the core product, including properties in the United States, South Korea and Australia, its theme parks and its video games development division (this work is now handled under licence by outside partners). He also laid down expectations for a shorter turn-

---

2. Weir, T. (27 June 2018) 'A Toy Story: LEGO, Aristotle, and the Business of Play'. (The Marketing Journal) Available at: http://www.marketingjournal.org/a-toy-story-lego-aristotle-and-business-of-play-todd-weir/

around of product development, and in order to show the company was still responding to trends and interests of its clients it developed product tie-ins with major brands, such as the highly successful 'Star Wars' line. The vision to ensure the core product remained a fascinating toy enjoyed by children was then translated into the company launching a performance-related pay scheme for the first time.

Fast forward four years and the company had returned to (significant) profit and in Britain, achieving 51% growth.

Achieving the crucial interplay between the mission and the contextual wisdom

For a new business or organisation, particularly one set up by someone with an entrepreneurial mindset, staying true to 'the business we are in' is a challenge when you need to generate income and establish yourself. In my first few years running my own business, Forum Strategy, there have been times when our organisation has been asked to diversify into work that, whilst attractive from a revenue point of view, didn't fit in with what I perceived to be our reason for being – supporting organisations (predominantly multi-academy trusts) to be innovative and creative in response to the challenges and opportunities they faced.

I remember once being asked to take on a marketing campaign for an organisation involved in the teacher supply agency sector. The contextual outside was placing a big emphasis on supply, because record numbers of teachers were leaving the profession, and supply agencies were proliferating. The contextual wisdom, on the face of it, was to do more work in this 'growth area' of teacher supply. However, my reference to the company's mission quickly made me stop in my tracks.

My view then, and now, is that a far more sustainable approach to covering staff absence is for schools to work together to create a small oversupply of permanently employed staff. These staff can then be deployed to work in a particular school when a member of staff is unwell or needs to take absence for other reasons. I felt this was a very innovative and important element of school-to-school partnerships, not least because the quality of teachers and support staff is so important.

It was clear to me that using teachers who were part of the organisation and had benefited from its training and performance management was a far better solution than a 'hired hand' for the day. Also, at a time of financial challenge and hardship in the education sector, I felt the costs of supply agencies were far too high in many cases. To take on the marketing services for a teacher supply agency would have been inconsistent with the business we were in, wouldn't have contributed to it either directly or indirectly, and therefore, despite the attractiveness of the retainer, was a 'no go'. My organisation's credibility and therefore its ability to provide good advice on the sustainable development of school partnerships would have been compromised. The contextual wisdom had to interplay with my company's sense of mission in order for me to understand how we would engage with the world of teacher supply – and it wasn't on the terms that were presented to me.

This is something every organisation goes through. Academy trusts are regularly asked to bid for grants – often by government – to deliver major initiatives that are of interest to the latest minister or mandarin. All too often, particularly in an era of tighter budgets, we see trusts bidding for money (which is attractive) with little reference to whether – given the commitment involved – this is right for the organisation. Taking on these initiatives may be financially attractive, but it inevitably takes focus, time and energy away from other things that may matter much more. A trust should be sure that the strategy is grounded in its why, the first foundation, and not an immediate response to a change in contextual weather – the policy agenda and the need for resources.

In Simon Sinek's work, the golden circle, he places the 'why' – the reason people get up in the morning to serve and work for an organisation – as central to its success in creating change and being a leader in its field. The CEO must come to the role fully subscribed to the board's mission or 'why' (or as I refer to it, 'the business we are in'), as this, together with how it relates to the context an organisation finds itself in, are the foundations of the vision they must deliver. The board is the guardian of the 'why' and the broader vision, and the CEO must understand that – as we will see in Chapter 3.

Foundation two: Contextual wisdom and knowing your meaningful outside

It is then from this point of clarity about the task ahead of them, and the environment around them, that a CEO can begin their journey to success. As the management guru Peter Drucker once said: 'on these two decisions what is our outside?' and 'what is our business?' – [rest] all the other work and all the other decisions inherent to being a CEO.' I would add foundations three and four – the foundation of a legacy mindset and the foundation of ethics and standards. But onto those shortly!

Unlike foundation one, 'the business we are in', this second foundation is the one that the CEO of a public organisation with a board can – and, indeed, should – play a key, but not a central or domineering, role in determining.

The board must draw on a wide-range of stakeholder perspectives, on research and trend analysis, and on horizon scanning, in order to apply contextual wisdom to its 'why' and therefore shape its vision for the time and context in which it finds itself.

But the CEO should be engaged as a key facilitator for the process of applying contextual wisdom because, as Lafley tells us, the CEO has a unique perspective on the organisation (seeing it all from above). They also – in most cases – have a day-to-day engrained knowledge of the sector and context within which they are operating.

I cover contextual wisdom in Chapter 3 where I look at the work the CEO must do to translate the vision into a compelling leadership narrative. However, as I say there, it is key for any CEO to be able to contribute to this foundation of the vision and have confidence that the board are involving them and listening to them on a regular basis. As the organisation progresses, the CEO must be continuously engaged in generating contextual wisdom in order to contribute to feeding their leadership narrative and developing strategy – but there will also be times where the contextual wisdom changes fundamentally. It is at this point that a CEO will need to engage their board and to ensure that the foundation is steadied and that the vision is revisited and carefully reviewed. Indeed, a CEO that does not identify and manage their role in this part of the process – given the pace of change many organisations are currently having to respond to – can quickly find themselves out of a job. Research by the Boston Consulting Group in 2018 said:

> 'During the past year, many global companies, for example China Petroleum and Coca-Cola, have named new CEOs. In many cases, this was because shareholders or the board felt that the previous leaders did not understand the massive disruptions facing their industries. These are not isolated events. Churn within many industries, due to incessant technological change, now means that leaders are being overtaken by their competitors at an unprecedented pace.'[3]

Key questions relating to foundations one and two

Are you absolutely clear on what business you are in (and what business you are not in)? This may seem an obvious question, but it has tripped many CEOs up – either because the board is not clear enough about what this is, or, the board has not engaged in the necessary dialogue with the CEO about the core sense of mission or 'why' at the heart of the organisation.

A CEO must ask if the board has clarified it, and, if they have, whether this is the business they themselves wish to be in! One thing a board must consider (as must a CEO who delivers on their behalf) is:

Is the focus too specific, potentially stifling your ability to innovate and shape the conditions for success?

Or, is it too wide and malleable, leading to undisciplined leadership and superficial attempts to develop new services and provision that may seem attractive or 'sexy', but are unrelated to 'the business you are in'?

Generating contextual wisdom. What is our outside? This question must be taken together with the previous one. What are the significant demographic, social, economic and political factors that will need to be reflected in turning the 'why' into a vision?

---

3. Bürkner, H, Faeste, L, Hemerling, J, Lyusina, Y & Reeves, M. (7 November 2017) 'The Transformations That Work – and Why'. (Boston Consulting Group) Available at: www.bcg.com/publications/2017/transformations-people-organization-that-work-why.aspx

The CEO and the board must be on the same page – where they are not, the relationship rarely lasts for long, not least because the outcome of this question forms the basis of the CEO's 'leadership narrative'. A CEO must, as we shall see, live and breathe the 'leadership narrative'.

When the board's view is different to the CEOs

In November 2018 it was reported that Ian Thomas, the CEO of Lewisham London Borough Council, had resigned after only seven months in the job. Thomas has impressively turned around inherent failures as Director of Children's Services for Rotherham Council. Only a short time after taking up post in Lewisham, the council's electoral make-up changed in an instant following an election, bringing a whole new agenda.

A spokesman for the council said that it had been decided to take a new direction and 'following a constructive dialogue with Ian' he had agreed to step aside from his role at the end of this year. Clearly the interpretation of the context (foundation two) had changed – new politicians entered with a different view of the world, and the subsequent interplay with the 'business we are in' changed the vision. The CEO's leadership narrative therefore had to change too. This, it seems, was enough for someone who had shown enormous leadership skills on his way to the CEO role to resign from the job only seven months in.

Foundation three: A legacy mindset

In identifying the vision and platform for the organisation's development, the CEO must have reference to the 'organisational mindset'. Is this an organisation where strategic leadership for the 'long game' is encouraged, or is it one that all too easily responds and reacts to the world around it? That can often depend on where the organisation is – is it responding to failure and in need of urgent improvement, or does it have a strong track record of success and needs to simply evolve and maintain its performance? However, even an organisation that is struggling and needs to improve rapidly cannot rebuild itself on sand. Long-term planning and a focus on sustainability is essential, not least in terms of the CEO's ability to focus on strategies that will reap rewards in the medium- to long-term.

As Lafley says, a successful CEO finds a balance between sufficient yield in the present and investment in the future. And be under no doubt, a CEO that achieves legacy is rarely an interim manager of one, two or maybe three years. A successful CEO is there for the long haul, with a mindset to plant and tend to their acorns so that they may cultivate a flourishing orchard. Research published by headhunters Korn Ferry in 2017 showed that whereas in the past, CEOs would have tenures close to the average, they now see more extremes for both shorter and longer tenures. There is a similar trend in academy trusts. No board wants a CEO who does not have the perseverance and strategic timeframe to move the organisation forward; improvement and transformation takes time to plan, execute and embed. Neither does a good CEO want to work with a board that has a short-term mindset and wants to implement 'quick fixes' without sustainability.

As the 2017 Korn Ferry report stated:

> 'Organizations must identify new CEOs who not only hit the ground running, but who also have the endurance to implement their plans. Boards of directors know tenure can be critical to the success of CEOs and organizations [...]. No company wants a CEO to flame out in the first few years. That disrupts and tarnishes the company—and it's expensive.'[4]

CEOs: Short-haul or long-haul executives?

There is no doubt that an organisation needs its CEO to be there for the long haul. But what happens when things don't go so well?

Organisations such as Uber, Reddit and Twitter have all at one time or another seen CEOs leave after just six months (in some cases, even less time). When it is so soon, it often comes down to a 'misalignment' of values or fundamental misunderstanding between the CEO and board. This is often the case where they are simply being asked by their boards

---

4. Korn Ferry Institute. (2017) 'CEO staying power'. Available at: www.kornferry.com/institute/download/download/id/18349/aid/1777

to pursue an agenda that they either don't agree with or don't feel cut out for. This is why conversations around foundations one and two are so important from the outset. CEOs and boards must not only discuss the terms and conditions of the CEO job, but also what success for the short and long-term looks like, what the organisation's interpretation of the 'contextual wisdom' is, and what the parameters of the organisation's agenda are in response. As the former CEO of Trent Academies Group, Phil Crompton, says: 'if you don't think you can work with the chair then for heaven's sake don't take the job. It will torture you both – and the organisation.'

Decisions to part ways beyond six months, but within a few years, are almost always down to underperformance on the part of the CEO or, indeed, exceptional performance by the CEO, which sees them being offered a better deal somewhere else. The former can be disappointing for both sides, and again depends on good relationships and a sound performance management process in order to be avoided or at least managed in the best interests of the organisation. The latter is always a risk, and it is why boards and CEOs must at all costs avoid embarking on a partnership that both sides are not wholly committed to and motivated to fulfil. A concept that is beginning to generate some interest is that where the CEO's first five years of salary are skewed – to a reasonable extent – towards the end of that period, making commitment and retention that bit more likely. Something for boards to ponder!

Football manager syndrome

CEOs can all too easily experience football manager syndrome. This is brought about when a board has short-term goals, with little time or tolerance for a diligent approach to put in place the foundations for long-term success. In any organisation, whether a football club, a schools' trust, or a public company, there will always be pressure for short-term results, and this pressure is often justified. Children get one shot, shareholders need to see returns, and demotion into another league can spell financial collapse.

However, this must be balanced. Success takes time to build. If we take two of the greatest sporting leaders of recent times, Sir Alex Ferguson (Manchester United in football) and Jean Todt (Scuderia Ferrari in grand prix racing), both took over five years to build their teams and shape a culture of success that lasted for well over a decade. Failure, or at least lack of success, was part of the course in those initial five years, with both bosses regularly seeing calls for their heads within the media and amongst fans. In both cases, their board resisted.

At the end of the 1989 football season, after finishing the season just above the relegation zone, Ferguson's time appeared to be up. At the final game the fans presented him with a banner that read 'Three years of excuses and it's still crap ... ta-ra Fergie'. Meanwhile Todt was under immense pressure, despite the millions provided by parent company FIAT and the signing of Michael Schumacher, the most talented and expensive driver in the world at the time. The team had failed to win either the drivers' or constructors' championship for five years following Todt's appointment. Failures of the car were often par of the course.

Yet, in both cases, the board held their nerve, giving the leaders the time, space and resources to build the foundations of success. Ferguson set about building a dream team of top-flight players whilst also redesigning the club's approach to scouting; all the while his board kept faith. As then Chairman Martin Edwards recalls: 'We never lost faith because we knew what Alex was trying to do at ground level [...]. We were patient, and just believing that we had got the right man but hoping like hell he was going to prove it to us.'[5]

The goals were long-term and the short-term gains were incremental at best. In time both Ferguson and Todt would be recognised as the greatest managers in their respective sports, with both achieving unprecedented and sustained success that had rarely been witnessed before. Building the team and culture takes time – particularly if the organisation is at a low ebb; and the CEO must have assurances from their board that they will be given the time to do so. That is not to say incremental gains needn't be made, they must. Both Todt and Ferguson demonstrated some quick wins, and the board must be assured that the organisation is going in the right direction, but there is an important lesson here: sustained successes and legacies take time to build.

---

5. Valente, A. (10 November 2017) 'Sir Alex Ferguson and Manchester United could easily have parted before success, says Martin Edwards'. (Sky Sports News) Available at: www.skysports.com/football/news/11667/11120791/sir-alex-ferguson-and-manchester-united-could-easily-have-parted-before-success-says-martin-edwards

The CEO can help to ensure the long-term mindset and bolster the confidence of the board by developing a five-year strategic business plan or corporate plan. This is best developed after at least three months in the role, and will help to provide a chartered course towards longer term sustained improvement and success. It may carefully reflect some of the six dimensions in this book, outlining strategies that carefully respond to the organisation's unique position and context. It will outline the vision, the range of strategies being put in place, a timeline in terms of the expected progress of those strategies, and some key objectives along the way. It is, essentially, the CEO's road map.

A business plan should, of course, evolve and change in response to changes in contextual wisdom and key developments within the organisation. It will be reviewed regularly and both executive and board should be open-minded to its on-going refinement. Ultimately, a CEO can use the dialogue and subsequent focus that a good corporate plan provides to ensure all stakeholders – not least the board – are not only fully engaged with and confident about the CEO's strategic approach, but also have a realistic view as to the timeframe for embedding strategies and securing sustainable progress. I cover the board and CEO's relationship around strategy further in Chapter 4.

Foundation four: Ethics and values

Finally, Lafley also wrote about the CEO's role in shaping the values and standards of the organisation. It must be remembered that the CEO's behaviour, the way in which they manage their key relationships internally and externally, how they use the resources at their disposal, and how they place an onus on long-term success and reputation in contrast to short-term quick wins, sets the tone for the rest of the organisation.

CEOs can easily compromise investment in key relationships and long-term strategy in order to 'handle' the pressures of the moment, and it is the values and standards they demonstrate that will define those experienced at every level of the organisation, as we will see in Chapter 5. Is this an organisation that places an onus on short cuts for short-term gain (ethical or not, legal or not), or an organisation that does the right thing in the short-term for long-term success?

Again, so much of this depends on the CEOs relationship with the board, and it is why any new CEO must choose their board as well as the board choosing them. Is the board focused on the short-term, or will the CEO have the support, backing, and targets that will enable them to balance the inevitable expectation of some 'quick-wins' and early progress with a focus on the long-term sustainability and success of the organisation? Indeed, the CEO should also consider whether they are aligned with the board in terms of values and ethics. Does the board demonstrate ethical leadership, 'living out' the right behaviours, or is it dominated by, say, conflicts of interests or obsessed by putting on 'a good face' for the outside world to achieve unsustainable growth? The CEO must be confident they have the board they and the organisation deserves. If there are fundamental misgivings, the CEO should move on.

Of course, ethical leadership begins with ourselves, knowing what we stand for and what we expect from others – including the board we intend to be accountable to. All CEOs, however, will be presented with decisions and choices at almost every turn that will require us to refer back to our ethics and values.

Marc Le Menestral suggests some quick tests to help us check whether we are possibly stepping over 'the line':[6]

1. The Sleeping Test: If I do this can I sleep at night?

2. The Newspaper Test: Would I still do this if it was published in a newspaper?

3. The Mirror Test: If I do this can I feel comfortable looking at myself in the mirror?

4. The Teenager Test: Would I mind my children knowing about this?

Ethics and values are not something that we write down and then leave behind while we're busy leading. The must be an integral part of our leadership and our leadership narrative. A good CEO will be ready to

---

6. Le Menestrel, M. (No date) 'Corruption and Obedience by Marc Le Menestrel'. (SlidePlayer) Available at: https://slideplayer.com/slide/9306146/

take the test above – almost every day – to ensure that they are living out and modelling such a key foundation of leadership.[7]

The link between the foundations of ethical leadership and the 'legacy mindset'

Some new CEOs have tripped up quite badly. This can be because stepping up to the role brings a pressure to demonstrate proficiency quickly. There is a temptation to cut corners, whether that means 'cooking the books or results' to impress investors or regulators, or to establish themselves amongst their peers by indulging in the perceived 'trappings of the job'.

Instead a new CEO must give themselves – and receive from their board – the time to establish themselves based on values, sustainable results and through a strategic outlook of what success can mean.

In the academy trust sector, we have seen a small minority of CEOs be accused of unethical behaviour, such as awarding themselves and companies they are involved with lucrative contracts on the side, or, in one case, allegations of using public funds to renovate a part-time holiday home! This is the most extreme and reprehensible behaviour, but it is almost always based on a need to prove oneself and one's status to others. It most often boils down to a lack of confidence, and, in the odd case, sheer greed. Whilst this behaviour reflects only a minority, the issue of lacking confidence and the temptation of focusing on short-term gain to prove oneself is something every CEO should be mindful of. It can come back to bite, and it can define the organisation's approach and mindset very quickly.

Lafley considers a long-term outlook to be harder for those who are newer to the role, and either lack the experience or confidence to focus on long-term strategic planning and objectives. He says 'first time CEOs rarely have much experience with weighing the balance toward a long-term future […]. Typically they've been accountable for results only a few months ahead […]. Their instincts for investing for long-term have not been honed. Those

---

7. It is important that all CEOs of academy trusts have reference to the new Framework for Ethical Leadership in Education: www.ascl.org.uk/policy/ascl-ethical-leadership-commission.html

instincts often arise from on-the-job training'.[8] A new CEO must be ready to have a discussion with their board about this and, through accessing mentoring from more experienced CEOs and by drawing on examples in leadership development literature, to develop the instincts and confidence for a longer-term view. This is essential to securing foundation three.

Taking a short-term view, to deliver results quickly, can lead to some real pressures that can quickly lead the CEO down a tricky path if they are not careful.

How does this relate to academy trusts?

The balance between short-term wins and long-term legacy building is a major challenge for academy trust CEOs and heads. Academy trust CEOs operate within a culture whereby annual results and expectations play a key part in how they are judged by government, and therefore by their boards. This can skew focus and investment on the short-term, but can also hamper a leader's ability to look ahead and consider how can more contextual issues, such as sustainable development of the organisation and curriculum reform that serves children for a changing economic and social landscape – can be addressed over the longer term. I am always astounded by how great an emphasis multi-academy trust (MAT) boards place on short-term indicators in CEO performance management process – often reverting back to the annual 'scores on the doors' as the overriding way of measuring success. It is the most forward thinking of boards that consider performance to have a broader interpretation – an interpretation that puts the longer-term needs of their end users, the pupils, and the organisation at the heart of the process.

Again, this shows how the legacy mindset depends fundamentally on clarity between board and CEO, particularly around foundations one and two: 'what business are we in?' and 'how do we engage with outside for contextual wisdom?' Some CEOs and trust boards may consider the scores on the doors as being the business they are in. That is a matter for the organisation, but it could be argued that it lacks enough scope for consideration of the contextual wisdom and the challenges and

---

8. Lafley, A, G. (2009) 'What Only the CEO Can Do'. (Harvard Business Review) Available at: https://hbr.org/2009/05/what-only-the-ceo-can-do

opportunities that this generation of children and young people currently face, and will face in the years ahead.

To go back to the analogy of the farmer, increasing numbers of MATs recognise the need to balance the short-term need for results and to succeed against government indicators (the weather), with a need to nurture the soil over time (build resources – teams of people and otherwise) and to carefully evaluate what they mean by 'the market' – their end users. Is the market they should serve the pupils or the politicians? A fairly obvious answer to many but one that, too often, becomes clouded.

This means rising above the short-term changes in the weather and looking to the longer-term trends and expectations of the people they ultimately serve, as well as investing in the development of people and resources for the future. As ever, the board, and the nature of the objectives it sets and the support it provides, determines the CEO's agenda.

In his speech to the Inspiring Leadership Conference in 2017, Steve Munby, the former CEO of the National College for School Leadership, and someone who I had the privilege of working with and advising over a number of years as a young special adviser, said this:

> 'Colleagues, I believe that the pressure on school and multi-academy trusts leaders to cross an ethical line is more challenging in England now than it has ever been. The combination of high accountability and high autonomy along with the lack of a 'middle tier' makes England's education system more extreme than almost any other in the world. This is what creates many of the moral dilemmas for school leaders, especially at times of austerity and at a time when many schools are struggling to recruit quality staff.

> 'Our high stakes accountability system places pressure on school leaders to behave in a way that maximises their performance as a school or MAT but may not always be in the best interests of the individual child or, indeed, of the wider community of schools. When you are fighting for the reputation of your school and every single inch of progress in learning is hard won, and in a system where falling below a floor target can cost you your job, it can

be tempting for our behaviours as leaders to drift away from the ethical line we perhaps ideally would want to take.'[9]

Wise words, and worth reflecting on.

A fifth foundation? Understanding the changing nature of the CEO role

My fifth foundation is about knowing the CEO role – its parameters, the influence it can have and where, and the barriers those in the role can face. This is as much about knowing what the role isn't, as what it is. Much of this will be covered in the following seven chapters as we review the six dimensions in turn. However, a CEO in 2019 must enter their role with their eyes open and understand that some of the pre-conceived ideas around the power and influence that comes with the role must be re-examined in the light of societal and technological change.

Much of what has been written so far in this opening chapter may appear timeless. As I have said before, we are talking about principles rather than prescriptive practices. However, we live in no ordinary times. Like everything and everyone else, CEOs and their organisations are having to respond to disruptive elements – for good or ill – that are having profound implications on concepts so fundamental as leadership, power, and influence.

Technology is the major disruptor. It is distributing power and influence, and it is putting organisations under unprecedented scrutiny. It is revolutionising everything, from how commerce is done, to how people (adults, professionals, young people and children alike) learn. It is revolutionising workplaces, as machines increasingly become more efficient and effective at performing routine tasks, and it is creating a level of transparency that puts leaders under unprecedented scrutiny. It presents countless risks and opportunities – in essence, it is a minefield for almost every CEO in every sector. Indeed, technology has changed people's attitude to power and position, with people feeling more empowered to participate in leadership and to challenge, without fear

---

9. Education Development Trust. (2018) *Steve Munby Inspiring Leadership 2017*
   [Video]Available at: https://vimeo.com/222313250

or hesitation, leaders in positions of relatively high authority. CEOs must recognise all of this and respond with a sense of positivity and opportunity.

Money, resources, titles and position still matter, but, with the pace and nature of societal and technological change as it is, they matter less than they did. Those CEOs who attach as much emphasis to these elements as in previous decades will become lost in their inability to secure a leadership narrative and a strategy that sticks in today's world.

The leadership coach, Shane Craddock, has recently written of how we are living in a time of 'VUCA', which stands for Volatility, Uncertainty, Complexity and Ambiguity. This is – for those CEOs struggling to adapt – causing unprecedented fatigue, stress and anxiety, as they struggle to know where to focus their efforts and exert power and influence to achieve success.

This makes the need to know 'what business we are in' even more important. That conversation with the board, on a regular basis, can provide the CEO with the clearest of navigation points – a rooted position from which to make sense of the world they are operating in and pursue the strategies that will have greatest impact.

What matters more than ever for the modern CEO is the ability to retain leadership and influence in an era where leadership and influence is being increasingly distributed. That requires them to engage, enthuse, inspire and co-create with those who are increasingly new partners in our leadership efforts. It's also about living the values in a world where congruency matters more than ever. The CEO's leadership narrative therefore – as we will see in Chapter 3 – must transcend the six dimensions of the role.

In their 2018 book *New Power*, Jeremy Heimans and Henry Timms state that 'the future will be a battle over mobilisation. The everyday people, leaders and organisations who flourish will be those best able to channel the participatory energy of those around them – for the good, for the bad, and for the trivial'. This reflects the fact that the CEO job is, more than ever, about focusing and facilitating the efforts of others, not only within but also beyond the organisation. This isn't just about technology. It is, as we will see later, about complexity and austerity. Most organisations no longer have the expertise or money to act in splendid isolation.

'The old command and control model of leadership is being replaced in the new digital era by a more adaptable and self-aware model. People are seeking more meaning, connection and engagement so the hierarchical and traditional approach to being a CEO and leader no longer works.' – Shane Cradock[10]

This requires the CEO to not only be aware of their personal limitations, but also the limitations of their organisations to influence and understand some of the complex dynamics and issues that will impact on their organisations. Currently, in the public sector, these organisational limitations are most often defined by money. However, the complexity of social change and the expanse of the knowledge economy means that both public and private sector organisations need to be outward facing. Being an organisation that galvanises others beyond it to contribute professional and social capital is essential and the CEO must – as the figurehead and as the person who sets the tone – spearhead this collaborative, interdependent mindset.

---

10. Cradock, S. (18 September 2018) 'The role of the CEO is changing – what does it take to become a great leader?' (Independent.ie) Available at: www.independent.ie/ business/in-the-workplace/the-role-of-the-ceo-is-changing-what-does-it-take-to-become-a-great-leader-37328576.html

The four foundations of the CEO role
Questions for reflection

ForumStrategy
Supporting organisations to plan, grow & thrive
All materials © Forum Education Limited 2018

1. Clarity

Are you and your board absolutely clear about (and agreed on) what business you are in, and what you are not in? Is this definition too narrow, too wide, or sufficiently broad enough to reflect the organisation's 'why'?

2. Contextual wisdom

Are you using your position of clarity to approach and interpret the 'meaningful outside' and gain contextual wisdom? Is this interpretation of the context and climate you are operating within informing your leadership narrative and strategies?

3. Legacy mindset

Is there a careful balance between cultivating the trees and planting the acorns? Does the board encourage a 'legacy mindset' for nurturing long-term success & sustainability, and avoid becoming overly absorbed with short-term goals & whims?

4. Values, ethics & standards

Are you ready to live and work in a way that is congruent with the standards and behaviours you/ your board expect of all those working within, and in partnership with, your organisation? Can you model this in all the actions & decisions you must take?

With the foundations secured and their interdependencies agreed, the vision and values are now clear – are you absolutely clear what the job of the CEO is, and what it isn't?

Chapter 2

The six dimensions of the CEO role

The four key pillars outlined in the previous chapter define the entire foundation of the CEO role. It is the interplay of foundations one, two and three that provide the vision, and foundation four that provides the values.

1. **Clarity of mission:** Our understanding of and focus on 'the business we are in, and the business we are not in', shared by the board.

2. **Contextual wisdom:** Our relationship and understanding of the 'meaningful outside' and how that influences the way in which we translate 'our business' into the context as it presents itself – responding to the weather, the resources, the people, and the needs and expectations of 'the market'.

3. **Legacy mindset:** Setting the balance between a focus on building sustainable organisational growth for the impact we desire in the long-term, with the (inevitable) need for short-term improvements and 'quick wins'.

4. **Ethics and standards:** The behaviours that we wish to embody and to model to the rest of the organisation. As CEO, people will follow your lead!

The fifth aspect I added from my reading of Lafley was the need for the CEO to be aware of what their role 'isn't'. That requires a clear understanding of what their role is and where the boundaries exist between their work and influence and, firstly, the work and influence of the board; secondly, the limitations of the law; and, lastly, the limitations of the resources at their disposal.

In Forum Strategy's work on organisational strategy and development, we have identified six areas that are key to sustainable growth and success. These six areas – being entirely strategic in nature – can be neatly reflected as six key dimensions of the CEO role, and are as follows:

The six dimensions of the CEO role:

1. Translating the vision into a compelling leadership narrative

2. Building an open, transparent and constructive relationship with the board

3. Being the Chief Talent Officer and the Culture Maker

4. Enabling improvement and innovation as an 'organisational habit'

5. Securing organisational sustainability and compliance

6. Fostering key relationships, building social and professional capital[11]

Translating the vision into a compelling leadership narrative. This is the focus of Chapter 3. The CEO must understand the interplay between 'the business we are in' – clarity about the 'why'; and how this is achieved, 'the how', through contextual wisdom. This is because this interplay forms the vision, and the vision must be translated by the CEO into a leadership narrative. The translation of the vision into a narrative that is engaging, inspiring and well understood will ensure that it then defines the other five dimensions completely.

Building an open, transparent and constructive relationship with the board. This will be covered in Chapter 4. It comes next because if there is a lack of complete understanding between the CEO and the board, the leadership narrative and the subsequent strategy will not stick. The

---

11. Forum Education Limited 2019

nature of the support, accountability/challenge, and backing that the CEO receives must align with the leadership narrative and be conducive to the subsequent strategy pursued by the CEO. If this is lost, the CEO will not get much further.

Being the Chief Talent Officer and the Culture Maker. This is the first truly fundamental aspect of strategic planning and delivery on the list and it is explored in Chapter 5. The success of an organisation can rarely exceed the talent and skills of its people – be it the chef in a restaurant, the designer at a fashion house, the lawyer stood out front in the court room, or the teacher in a classroom. The successful CEO knows that their ability to shape an organisational culture that attracts, trains, and retains high quality people will define their leadership – for good or ill. For many, it is a challenge to understand their role and influence in this regard, particularly where they lead a large organisation and could be considered to be quite remote from the frontline.

Enabling improvement and innovation as an 'organisational habit'. This is the focus of Chapter 6. The CEO has a unique perspective of overall organisational performance and must create the conditions that enable a culture of continuous improvement and performance at scale. The CEO must not drive that improvement personally. Personally, to do so would be to create an organisation that is dependent on the CEO, rather than one whose success (or path to it) is firmly embedded within the culture. The CEO's job is to make sure the seven pillars of improvement at scale are in place and that improvement becomes an 'organisational habit' – this is the recipe for sustained success. The seven pillars are: vision for improvement; capacity; collective commitment; real time and robust intelligence; process and project management; research and innovation; and quality assurance.

Securing organisational sustainability and compliance. This is the focus of Chapter 7. In an age of austerity for so many organisations and unprecedented complexity, brought about by social and demographic changes as well as technology, how can the CEO ensure that they are running an organisation that has an 'investor mentality'? That is, focused on 'achieving substantiality dividends' for the organisation on its investment in staff, new services, new resources, and its research and innovation projects. The temptation for many in these tight financial and uncertain times is to lead a bean counter organisation – but this goes against the foundation of 'legacy mindset' discussed in Chapter 1. Complexity and change also presents key risks to running a compliant organisation – something that no CEO should underestimate.

Fostering key relationships, building social and professional capital. This is the focus of Chapter 8. The role of the CEO is to generate professional and social capital. This means forging the strategic relationships necessary to bring about the knowledge, improvement, innovation, and support necessary to move an organisation forward. Again, in an age of austerity and complexity, leaders and organisations cannot operate alone – they need help; and help only comes through positive, aligned, accountable, and sustainable partnerships. The risk for any leader is that they get collaborative overload, not least through a failure to prioritise and focus on the relationships that have the greatest bearing on success and where they can have the most influence.

Each of these six dimensions will be covered in the following chapters, as will the fourth foundation, 'the importance of ethics', modelling the standards and behaviours that we expect from ourselves and from others.

Chapter 3

Translating the vision into a compelling leadership narrative

'Reaching for the world, as our lives do, as all lives do. Reaching that we may give the best of what we hold as true. Always it is by bridges that we live.'

– Phillip Larkin

It is a misnomer that the CEO sets the vision. They don't. Beware the leader who talks about 'my vision'. In any organisation, it is the board that is responsible for setting the vision with reference to the CEO and a wide range of stakeholders (not least the people the organisation serves).

The CEO should play an active and constructive part in forming the vision, but not a central one. Indeed, the only exception to this is an organisation where the CEO is also 'the owner'. However, even in this case, setting the vision without reference to your 'meaningful outside' – your end users and trusted advisers – means that you may be in the business you want to be in, but it will be a vision that lacks contextual wisdom. You would then run the risk of having a vision that is potentially irrelevant to anyone else, and, in such a case, the enterprise is essentially a hobby!

As I touched on in Chapter 1, it is within these visioning discussions that the board must do three things:

1. Agree 'what business we are in' – the why of the organisation.

2. Draw upon contextual wisdom to consider how 'the business we are in' relates to the world around us – drawing on a deep understanding of the landscape and a connection to those they serve. The 'business we are in' may need to be revisited so that it relates to context (as didn't happen with Blockbuster), but without becoming too heavily influenced and redefined by external 'trends' as to become lost (as we saw with Lego).

3. Have a 'legacy mindset', focused on the long-term goals and achievements of the organisation and how these can be sustained over time.

Three elements of a compelling vision

Clarity: What is 'the business we are in'?

Vision

Context: What is 'the meaningful outside'?

Legacy: The 'long game' over the short term

ForumStrategy
Supporting organisations to plan, grow & thrive

© Forum Education Limited 2018

An example of good visioning from the multi-academy trusts sector is where the board quickly comes to the conclusion that the business they are in is 'giving every child the very best start in life, with the academic qualifications and the personal development and values necessary to thrive and succeed in their future lives'. That is quite a clear statement about the business we are in. However, whilst being noble and certainly engaging, it could be written in the 19th, 20th or 21st century. It is rather too abstract to form a vision. This is a mission statement – the 'business we are in'.

A good trust board should then ask the question, with reference to their end-users (pupils and parents), businesses, staff, local community groups and others – 'what is our meaningful outside? What is the context we are operating in and how does that interplay with the business we are in?' This is where contextual wisdom comes to the fore, and this is the element of the visioning process that the CEO should certainly not be excluded from.

In our work with academy trusts, we know that by exploring some of the barriers and opportunities that their end-users currently face – within the current context as they experience it, trusts are able to achieve a more meaningful vision that relates to and connects with people's day to day experiences. The focus moves from the warm words of a noble mission to a commitment (or series of commitments) of sufficient substance and direction that is tangible and powerful enough for people to relate to and motivate them to do really great things.

In 2019, the all-pervading influence of technology and the changing nature of the world of work is redefining, to an extent, what academic success for pupils should look like. Likewise, the growing challenges around mental health, the rise of childhood obesity, the increasing economic uncertainty affecting households through the gig economy, and the impact of austerity, is all influencing what is meant by successful personal development. Dealing successfully with uncertainty and adversity is essential to personal development. An organisation that wishes to have an impactful strategy needs a vision and a leadership narrative that not only deeply connects with its own end-users' and staffs' daily experiences and realities, but also connects to those others beyond the organisation who the CEO will need to involve and mobilise in order to achieve the mission and vision. This is where the 'bridges' between the idea of success and the reality in which it is realised begin to be formed. This clarity of vision is so crucial for CEO to be able shape their leadership narrative in a way that connects with those both within and beyond the organisation.

So, for academy trusts, 'the business we are in' – the sense of mission – could possibly evolve into a vision that reads along the following lines: 'we want to give all our pupils the best start. Academically, we want them to be highly literate, and to access learning opportunities that prepare them for a changing, highly flexible economy and ensure they are masters rather than servants of technology. In terms of personal development, we want them to be both physically and mentally healthy, with the resilience, adaptability and values to make the right choices and build successful relationships.' It is at this point that a tangible vision emerges from the mission, a vision that can quite easily be translated into a leadership narrative and into strategy.

The CEO's role

The CEO as a sector expert (usually), and the person who will lead the agenda, must have a say. But, it is for the board, first and foremost, to adopt and own the vision.

This is a crucial stage for a CEO. They will either walk into an organisation with a clear vision set by the board (not unheard of) or walk into an organisation that is in the process of revisiting, or about to revisit, its vision and wants the CEO to have some involvement in the process. The former is often an easier position for a prospective CEO to find themselves in as they can quickly decide if this is the organisation for them and whether they have the skills and experience necessary to execute the boards wishes before committing. The latter may tell of a board that needs direction; OK to a certain extent, as its good to involve the CEO to a degree, but not good if the ship is drifting and the CEO is expected to set the destination. This has too often been the case in academy trusts, for example. Yet the resulting lack of accountability, support or understanding provided by the board is ultimately damaging and the CEO is at best lonely, and, at worst, completely left to their own devices. It is not unusual in this case for the CEO to essentially write their own job description and performance management targets. There's no wonder ethical issues have arisen in some academy trusts.

The imperfect analogy of politics

Consider the Prime Minister (PM) as CEO of a democratic country – the country is their board. The electorate does not accept its politicians setting out a vision for the country after they had been elected; they instead expect to provide a mandate to the party that best made a case to the country about how it could best be served. The same should be the case for a CEO, who is given the mandate by their board.

It's not a perfect analogy, an electorate is consulted by political parties – headed by a prospective PM – who come to them with a fully formed vision (a manifesto) for the electorate's endorsement or otherwise. In a company or organisation, a board should draft the vision in consultation with their stakeholders. In either case, be you a CEO or Prime Minister, you are there to execute a mandate chosen by others either at the ballot box or following a visioning process led by a board.

A CEO must think like a good Prime Minister, knowing their constituents (the board) have placed great power, but also responsibility, in their hands.

Some people, I know, will see the omnipotent CEO as normal. There are CEOs out there who see their boards as something to tolerate, who believe it is their job to set the vision, and to be left alone to get on with it free from the direction or accountability of a board. Some CEOs bring this expectation from previous roles and can be left shocked when they find – quite rightly – they are very accountable to a board with a strong sense of direction. My clear view, which is consistent with corporate governance and the very language used to describe the CEO role, is that the CEO is there to execute the will of the board. They are the Chief 'Executive' Officer. For the best CEOs, having a board with a strong sense of direction whilst also providing the requisite challenge and support to help the CEO pursue that agenda is seen as being essential.

Indeed, recent research by Russell Reynolds Associates, and featured in Harvard Business Review, found that an ability to prioritise and focus on substance, rather than traits traditionally associated with the role such as self-promotion and extroversion, were key to a CEO's success.[12] A good board with a clear vision that stays true to the organisation's mission yet translates it to context, will give the CEO the mandate they need to prioritise and focus on substance; the narrative and strategy required.

That said, a good board will not be looking for a 'push over' either. Recent research featured in Harvard Business Review stated that: 'When a board wants to increase their odds of hiring a successful leader, it should interview and assess candidates for intensity and impatience, find those who focus on core issues, and search for a leader with the ability to have a point of view while still being open-minded and recognising the power of the organisation around him or her.'[13] Knowing that they are there to 'execute' the boards vision, but that they must do so with intensity and focus and, yes – to have a point of view in informing that vision, is the delicate but important position that boards and their CEOs must strive for.

The egotistical leader will not like some of this, but a CEO must – particularly in 2019 – be a good listener, a good learner, a willing but respectful contributor, and defer to the accountability systems that keep them in check. I'll come back to all of this in Chapter 4.

In any case, the CEO must fully buy into and own the vision, not least because their performance targets and their own motivation to do an extremely challenging job, will rely on it.

Hints and tips for CEOs on how they engage with setting the vision:

- **Don't lead this**. Be a very willing and engaged participant, with a constructive point of view. Within these parameters, be as active as the board allows you to be. They must respect and listen to your views, but be ready for (and encourage them with)

---

12. Stamoulis, D. (15 November 2016) 'How the Best CEOs Differ from Average Ones'. (Harvard Business Review) Available at: https://hbr.org/2016/11/how-the-best-ceos-differ-from-average-ones
13. Ibid.

the drawing in of a wide range of stakeholders and advisers – not least your organisation's end users. The board must be clear on 'the why' – the business we are in, but they will need your help and that of others in accessing the contextual wisdom necessary to create a compelling vision. This work is the foundation of your role, but you shouldn't have huge influence in it.

- **Facilitate the involvement of a wide-range of participants.** You will know your sector or industry well so help your trustees to engage with it, including people with expertise such as researchers, analysts and policymakers. You will also want to give your staff the confidence to inform the vision, without fear or favour. Do not stand in the way of this; encourage and facilitate it by working closely with the board to do so.

- **Encourage the board to be as clear as possible about their vision for the organisation.** You don't want them to 'over define' the strategies to achieve it, but you don't want abstract niceties either. Push for them to set a vision that has clear direction and sufficient substance, grounded in the contextual realities your organisation finds itself in, so that you can take it forward knowing exactly what success looks like and what you need to do to get there.

- **Ensure that the vision is your reference point for your performance management discussions.** The discussion about performance targets should be a two-way conversation initially, with the board taking the final decision as to what your targets and goals are. The ability to focus and prioritise what matters is essential to the CEO role.

As my former colleague and a regular contributor to Forum Strategy programmes, Vanni Treves CBE (a former Chair of Channel 4 and Equitable Life) tells us: 'the executive should understand what his or her board is there to do and wants to do and the ways in which it wants to do it, and then make it happen – all within the bounds of what is possible!'

That is the premise upon, and the parameters within, which the CEO should forge their all-important leadership narrative.

Translating the vision into a leadership narrative

It is through the interplay between the 'business we are in', the application of this within current 'contextual wisdom' and the legacy mindset (foundation three) that the vision for the organisation is forged.

The CEO should then bring this to life for the organisation and its stakeholders by forging a compelling leadership narrative, their interpretation of how the organisation can fulfil its vision within the context it finds itself in. The CEO's job is to deliver upon 'our organisational vision', using the leadership narrative they forge to drive strategy and to mobilise people, resources and systems to achieve the outcomes that represent the board's definition of success.

As the leadership thinker, Stephen Denning writes, the translation of the vision into the leadership narrative must be compelling and all pervading:

'Once a commitment is made, the goal will seem larger, bolder, and more exciting... leaders need to fix on it like a laser beam. They need to see it intensely, even obsessively. They feel it. They hear it. They taste it. They smell it. It becomes part of them, their very identity, because it is something they are committed to make happen, come what may, whatever it takes.' – Stephen Denning, *The Secret Language of Leadership*

The leadership narrative is the glue that holds the CEO's agenda together and pervades the organisation; motivating people, driving day-to-day decisions, and providing the reference point for the organisation's external relationships and communications. On joining an organisation or stepping up to the role, it is almost inevitable that the CEO, whilst understanding that the mission and vision are set by the board – will want to develop their own, unique, leadership narrative and therefore strategy. It is extremely unusual for a CEO (unless it is an interim or caretaker CEO) to stick to their predecessor's narrative and strategy. What works for one person will not work for another.

In essence, a leadership narrative has an overarching theme articulating the destination and course of the organisation through stories, including the lives and experiences of our end users. The narrative builds upon how these can be improved and enhanced by the organisation, the experiences of staff and examples of impact and excellence (as well as frustrations), the organisation's relationship with the world around it, and short to medium-term goals and accomplishments that act as signposts along the way. The important thing is that this narrative is aligned with the vision and articulates or reflects the strategies that will enable the organisation to get where it needs to be. This all takes time, especially for a CEO that is new to the organisation.

In developing their leadership narrative, the CEO should try to ensure that it meets a number of key criteria:

- **It affirms 'the business we are in'.** What we are about, and – crucially – what we are not about.

- **It reflects the 'meaningful outside'** and is based on contextual wisdom, the daily experience of followers, staff and stakeholders alike. It connects with people's experience of life and the world in which they live – not simply the work and tasks to be done. The CEO must keep listening to bring this and the work to life – the great storyteller is, first of all, a great listener.

- **It is, therefore, inclusive.** This isn't the CEOs' story, it is the organisation's and its people's story. It is about 'us' not 'I'. It invites continued participation and ownership amongst our followers.

- **But, it is authentic.** It has the CEO's personal stamp on it, they are – after all – the lead player and it aligns with their own motivations, aspirations and experiences.

- **It tells the story of 'a journey to something better'.** Providing a clear image in people's minds of what the destination looks like in the long-term. It is strategic and inclusive. It is about being on a meaningful journey together, not reactive to events or placing an onus on short-term operational gains needed by management. It carefully reflects the legacy mindset.

- **It connects to every facet of the business and the people's experience of work too.** Not necessarily explicitly, but certainly implicitly. This can be achieved by including tangible goals and stepping-stones to success, that people can relate to and feel connected to through their daily work.

- **It reflects the ethics, values, standards and behaviours the organisation stands for.** A narrative based on doing things 'right' as well as 'well'.

These tests are important for CEOs. They need the narrative to not only inspire and inform, but to be 'lived out' by everyone with a role in taking the organisation forward. Strategies only, after all, become a reality through people and their behaviours and relationships. The most important aspect, beyond ethics, is how the narrative connects to people. A good story always draws the audience into the narrative. The connection is everything.

The CEO as 'communicator in chief'

In my early career I was a speechwriter and public affairs manager for CEOs and politicians. I enjoyed the role because it involved being close to the heart of things and writing about issues I cared about – be it education, tackling poverty or community cohesion. However, I also quickly began to realise how crucial my role was to the CEO in helping them to translate the vision into a narrative that was essential to informing and motivating their people and encouraging the right kind of behaviours and standards of work. The story of the organisation had to be told, and it was told through a compelling narrative that connected to people's hopes, interests and aspirations; both for themselves and the people they worked with and on behalf of.

The best leaders I have worked with, whether they are CEOs, senior politicians, or school leaders, have always placed high value on communications. A good leader will use storytelling well. Our love of storytelling is engrained within us, because for the generations before radios, televisions, and mobile phones, it was the only source of entertainment. It is storytelling that ensured the survival and progress of humanity, through the education and wisdom they transferred from one generation to the next. There's no wonder that we humans love it! And there's no wonder that the best CEOs are particularly good at it.

This doesn't mean to say that the CEO needs to be an extrovert leader. A loud, self-promoting CEO can also lack the authenticity and the ability to listen that shapes their leadership narrative. People can disconnect. I have seen CEOs that have fallen into the trap of making big speeches – delivered with great fanfare – but not having spent the time listening to or understanding their audience's point of view first. This is why the great CEO spends time listening in the first few months of the role, understanding the hopes, interests and aspirations of those that work for them and those they serve. They acquire stories, they begin to recognise stories of their own lives that relate to others, and – eventually – they begin to forge a leadership narrative for the organisation.

In his book *The Secret Language of Leadership*, Stephen Denning talks about the need to connect with audiences first if they are to 'hear' the leader's story: 'If leaders are going to have any success in prompting the audience to discover this new story and imagine a different kind of future, they first need to understand the current story that their listeners are living. What's going on in that world? How does it hang together? Why does the world that people are currently living in make sense? What is it about their attitudes, beliefs, hopes, dreams and fears that makes that world fit together in a way that is broadly plausible?'

I once worked with a CEO who had spent the first few months of the role either on the telephone to or visiting, clients or in meetings with staff – gauging views, understanding their perspectives and experiences, and asking for their views on the market the organisation was in and how the organisation could better respond. This is all-important communication, and it makes for a more informed, and more inclusive and authentic leadership narrative because it is based on a genuine understanding of their clients' and colleagues' lives. It allows the CEO, over time, to forge the leadership narrative that everyone can relate to.

Similarly, a politician I worked for insisted on spending every Friday in the community at schools, local businesses, in shopping centres and in cafes; just asking questions and listening, never pontificating or selling. The people's story became his story and in him they saw themselves; their hopes, their interests and their aspirations. The leadership narrative was forged with substance and grounded in reality. But neither leader forgot the business they were in and what they were there to do, to lead and achieve results.

One CEO I know, who leads a hospital trust, talks about the importance of 'authentic connections' when meeting with their teams and customers/end users. In the early days of his role he took to making pre-planned visits to the hospital wards. On arrival, after sometimes weeks of anticipation, he would find his hospital managers and ward managers would meet him at the door, ready to chaperone him around the ward while inviting him to meet with select patients who were all too aware of his impending visit. This CEO would soon come to describe these visits as 'Royal Visits' and quickly found that they told him very little about the experiences of patients or the delivery of services. The hospital staff, understandably, were putting on their best efforts to impress the CEO.

In time, he took a very different approach, asking to join staff in what he describes as 'the thick of it', attending random meetings, surgeries, and live consultations (providing notice but asking staff not to plan in any way for his attendance) and walked the corridors of his hospitals without prior warning. Only this way did he feel he got to the heart of patients' and staff experiences and a sense of the real stories within the organisation he led. The conversations he had and the observations he made were the building blocks of an authentic, inclusive and relevant leadership narrative. People saw their own concerns, successes, ideas, and aspirations reflected in the leader's narrative.

In contrast I spent two years working with a politician who had forgotten all of this. I began working for him at the end of his career, a senior figure who had seemingly forgotten who had put him there; a loyal constituency of voters. He enjoyed the company of the political and social elite. His view of the electorate gradually become one of frustration – 'they always complain about things', he said, 'we're doing a good job.' His attitude reflected the decline of the New Labour government and the view amongst the electorate that it had lost touch, its narrative in its autumn years becoming a defence of policy and the attacking of its opponents (both on the other side of the chamber, but just as fiercely between party factions), not one that reflected the reality of people's day to day lives.

This complete disconnect was exposed so glaringly when the then Prime Minister, Gordon Brown, visited voter Gillian Duffy on the campaign trail ahead of the 2010 general election. Duffy set out her concerns on a range of issues from immigration to crime and pensions. Just minutes after leaving her home, Brown was overheard, on a microphone that had been inadvertently left on, dismissing her as a 'bigoted woman'. When the news came out during an interview later that day, Brown was pictured with his head in his hands as the tape was played. The wise and experienced politician that he was, Brown knew that he had pretty much lost the election from that moment on.

Indeed, there was nothing compelling or inspiring about the politician I worked for or his colleagues in 2010. That was because there was no leadership narrative, just a group of politicians on the defence, citing former glories and dismissing an electorate that it seemed to consider inferior. The electorate had its say, with David Cameron marginally gaining the support to establish an alternative 'coalition' government just a few days later.

It was clear that Brown and his cabinet had failed in many ways to 'stay alive' to the world, to see the world, as it were, through the eyes of the new, enthusiastic, and grounded politicians they once were. The decline of the New Labour government (although some would not call it that by 2008/09) was stark because when the party came to power in 1997 it was on the crest of a wave, seemingly representing the 'spirit of the times' and connecting with the electorate's deepest hopes and aspirations. As Blair said in his memoirs, such was the scale of Labour's landslide victory that he thought he had done something 'unconstitutional'. How easily a leader and their organisation can lose touch after some time in power. Once they do, the leadership narrative can quickly become unstuck.

How does this apply to leadership of multi-academy trusts?

A key focus for many MAT CEOs is the growth and sustainability of their trusts. So much so, in fact, that it has fed into their leadership narrative. More often than not when asked to describe their trusts, a CEO will revert to the number of schools they have and the Ofsted grades of those schools. Their leadership narrative, to go back to the farming analogy, is quickly eclipsed by today's weather and the resources at our disposal. However, this is far from of interest to those they lead or serve; their staff, parents or pupils. The end-users do not care about the weather today or the resources at your disposal. They care about who you are, why you do what you do, and how you relate to them. They want and need to connect with their leaders.

Growth is in fact just a strategy that should sit beneath and serve a greater leadership narrative, not a leadership narrative in itself. In fact, deep down, for many CEOs, the quest for growth is driven by the fact that it can open up resources and collaboration that facilitates better learning and development outcomes for all children. The problem for many CEOs trying to build professional and social capital amongst those they lead is when the expansion of the organisation becomes growth for its own sake and puts those outcomes at risk (again, as we have too often seen).

In his book, Stephen Denning quotes the psychologist Dan McAdams who says:

> 'People carry with them and bring into conversation a wide range of self-stories and these stories are nested in larger and overlapping stories, creating ultimately a kind of anthology of the self. Although no single story may encompass all of the many narratives that any given person can use to make sense of his or her life, some stories are larger and more integrative than others and come closer, therefore, to functioning as identify formats for a given person. Thus, identity may not be captured in a single grand narrative for each person, but identity, nonetheless, is accomplished through narrative.'[14]

The CEO should not confuse their position at the top of the organisation with a permit to no longer need to engage with and listen to those on the 'frontline' of their organisations. In fact, they must 'step up' their role in engaging, discussing, seeking views, and, yes, informing others at all levels also. Of course, it is impossible for a CEO to connect with everyone in their organisation in a meaningful way or to know everyone's names. However, the CEO must ensure they have meaningful meetings and interactions, in context, with as wide a range of people as possible. This invitational approach is the nourishment for their leadership narrative and it is also one of the best platforms for sharing it.

---

14. McAdams, D. P. (2001) 'The Psychology of Life Stories', *Review of General Psychology*, 5, pp. 100-122.

Staying alive to the world around us: the learner in chief

As the person at the top of the organisation, and undoubtedly at the highest trajectory of their career, the CEO could easily fall into the role of 'expert in chief'. Yet, this is probably the greatest danger any CEO could fall into. Most will have made the step from expert in their field – the specialist leader who has reached the top through their knowledge, experience and ability to make the right leadership and managerial decisions by drawing from within. This is probably the hardest transition to make. The CEO is no longer 'expert in chief' and must become 'learner in chief'.

As David Strudley, former CEO of Acorns and Rainbows Children's hospices, says humility is the key to being a good CEO, looking to the expertise and knowledge of the team of experts around you to make the right decisions, because you are no longer the expert in the room. Your role is to bring wisdom – an ability to understand everyone's roles well enough, whilst applying strategic insight and leadership.[15]

That is why the CEO can never be considered the 'expert' and must be continuously open to the opportunities, perils and interdependencies of the world around them. The experts are looking for a leadership narrative through which to apply their expertise and the CEO must provide that, but they can only provide that by being 'alive' to the organisation and the wider world around them. Questioning, questioning and questioning in order to gain that insight that keeps their narrative relevant, honest and fresh.

Albert Einstein famously said: 'Don't think about why you question, simply don't stop questioning. Don't worry about what you can't answer, and don't try to explain what you can't know. Curiosity has its own reason. Aren't you in awe when you contemplate the mysteries of eternity, of life, of the marvellous structure behind reality? And this is the miracle of the human mind – to use its connections, concepts, and formulas as tools to explain what man sees, feels and touches. Try to comprehend a little more each day. Have untold curiosity.'

---

15. Forum Strategy. (2018) *Leaders In Conversation: Episode 2 – David Strudley CBE* [Video] Available at: www.youtube.com/watch?v=Scr3AArGaTE

A CEO lacking confidence or misunderstanding their role will be struck by the words above. The tendency to worry about what we can't answer in leadership roles is one of the greatest barriers to authentic, strategic leadership that confronts the hard questions. Yet it exists within so many CEOs who then fail to be invitational and create an inclusive leadership narrative that both motivates and draws upon the wisdom of those around them, both within the organisation and beyond it. This is another example where the CEO should take a 'step back' to step forward. They must be sufficiently vulnerable.

In a recent article for Harvard Business Review, Curt Nickisch wrote:

'The human trait of curiosity is universal in children. But it's less common in adults and often hard to find in the workplace. The fear being that curiosity cripples your career by leading you out of line. However, new research shows that curiosity can drive an organization's performance. It improves engagement and collaboration and inspires novel solutions.'[16]

The CEO sets the tone here. Curiosity is essential to developing their leadership narrative and it is essential to creating an engaged, collaborative and innovative organisation. My three-year-old daughter sometimes asks questions that I simply do not have the answers to, such as why are words like 'right' and 'leaves' pronounced the same way but have completely different meanings? I do not know, but what I do know is that I have got to accustomed to the idea very quickly and I've never thought to question it! She will begin to lose some of that innate curiosity as she reaches the ages of five and six, that is inevitable, but the degree to which she loses it will certainly define her ability to make the right decisions and choices in her life.

One of the great things about Forum Strategy's five regional CEO networks in England is that they are about cross-sector learning. CEOs tell me that the opportunity to meet with and hear from people doing 'the same' job, but in other sectors, sits amongst some of the best professional learning they have experienced. This is, I feel, because CEOs let down their guard when working with peers in other sectors. They feel, because

---

16. Nickisch, C. (9 October 2018) 'The Power of Curiosity'. (Harvard Business Review) Available at: https://hbr.org/ideacast/2018/10/the-power-of-curiosity.html

they are from different worlds, that they don't need to demonstrate expertise on the subject matter or an encyclopaedic knowledge of the policy environment or the strength of their relationship with the latest minister, for example. They are simply making connections without the pressure of being seen to be asking naïve questions. In fact, as we know, it is often those questions that provide the most enlightening answers.

The world around us is full of assumptions and ideas, opportunities and challenges, all too often overlooked or missed as we go about our busy days, trying to appear as competent and prepared for the task in hand as possible. Of course, we do need to be competent, but we must also be able to embrace a mindset where questioning and learning are 'the norm'. There is strength rather than weakness in this. For the CEO, being 'alive' to the world around them is essential to their narrative and their strategy. Yet the busyness of their lives is such that time for reflection, for reading and for questioning is often pushed to the bottom of the list. Both listening and CPD is even more essential when a person becomes a CEO than it was when they were a senior manager.

In his book *The Ten Commandments for Business Failure*, former president of Coca-Cola, Donald R. Keough suggests that the failure of businesses stems from a number of leadership actions – of which four link directly to a lack of curiosity: not taking risks; being inflexible; isolating themselves; assuming infallibility; not staying true to their principles; not taking time to think; putting all their faith in outside experts and consultants; loving bureaucracy; sending mixed messages; being afraid of the future; and above all, losing their passion for their work and for life.

What can CEOs do to remain insatiable learners?

- Spend time at the frontline, but not on 'royal visits' (try to set aside an hour or two every week).
- Read beyond the sector – particularly on economic, social and technological developments.
- Embrace the challenge and guidance of their board.
- Create 'staff forums' where people can openly discuss the key issues facing the organisation with a greater sense of 'parity'.

- Meet with their senior team once a month or so in a more informal context beyond the work environment (one CEO I know cooks a curry for their team).
- Access networking opportunities with CEO peers both within and beyond your own sector.
- Access the support of a mentor (see Chapter 8).

Investing time in curiosity

It is imperative that CEOs create the space to walk the corridors of their schools, engage with their communities, and build relationships with strategic partners such as businesses, third sector organisations, researchers, politicians and civil servants. Reading is also important, not simply the generic leadership manuals and government guidance (important though this is), but also books and articles that allow us to identify trends in society and in the economy – the things that our children, young people and, indeed, our staff, need us to make sense of. CEOs must be avid relationship builders and avid readers, playing the role of lead learner all the time.

A study by Harvard Business review that tracked the time allocation of 27 CEOs for a full quarter (three months) each, found that CEOs generally struggled to carve out 'alone time' for thinking and reflection. This is hugely concerning. CEOs spent 28% of their work time alone, on average – but again, that varied a great deal, from a low of 10% to a high of 48%. Much of this was fragmented into blocks of one hour or less, with the research concluding that 'CEOs need to cordon off meaningful amounts of alone time and avoid dissipating it by dealing with immediate matters, especially their in-boxes.'[17]

As we have seen, in a 21st century defined by pace, technology, complexity and uncertainty, a CEO cannot be expected to be an 'island of wisdom'. It is simply impossible. A CEO should – in forging and sustaining their leadership narrative – ask the hard questions, both of themselves and quite openly through the narrative itself. They must involve the crowd,

---

17. Porter, M & Nohria, N. (2018) 'How CEOs Manage Time'. (Harvard Business Review) Available at: https://hbr.org/2018/07/the-leaders-calendar

draw on their wisdom, and – most of all – learn. As Einstein says, they must have untold curiosity.

Indeed, when recently asked about the way in which technology was shaping his thinking, Hikmet Ersek, CEO of money transfer services company Western Union, said 'it's not sitting in the corner office having an idea about technology. It's really about listening to the customer and adapting that technology to their needs, you need to listen to the voice of the customer to be successful.'[18] The leadership narrative is more malleable than the mission and vision of the organisation. It has to be. It is up to the CEO to make sure that, through being the 'learner in chief', inviting others through questions, discussion, contemplation and co-creation – the leadership narrative is inclusive, relevant and motivating. We will look more closely at this as we consider the importance of social and professional capital later in this book.

As well as setting the narrative and having the humility necessary to make the right calls, the CEO is also, as I have said elsewhere, the most important person in facilitating the board's access to contextual wisdom. CEOs must be enthusiastic futures-thinkers and must be able to anticipate the opportunities and challenges that await their organisations and those they serve. How do they develop and adapt their strategy in response? This means listening, learning, and constantly scanning the horizon. This is why it is so important for us that every member CEO of our MAT leaders networks receives a weekly strategic bulletin of key developments, and a number of trust boards and leadership teams also subscribe to this service.

The influence of the leadership narrative on strategy

The leadership narrative defines the other five dimensions of the CEO role (as we will see later in greater detail) in the following ways:

The relationship between the trust board and the CEO. The trust board will wish to see their vision brought to life, with it having traction within and beyond the organisation. A strong and effective leadership narrative links vision to organisational delivery and behaviour, and it is the job of the CEO to achieve this.

18. KPMG. (2018) 'Leading from the centre'. (KPMG) Available at: https://assets.kpmg/content/dam/kpmg/uk/pdf/2018/05/KPMG-CEO-Outlook-2018-UK.pdf

The Chief Talent Officer and Culture Maker. People want to work for organisations they feel a deep sense of connection to, and that give their lives and work deeper purpose and legacy. This is certainly the case for the new generation of workers (millennials and Gen Z's) who place the purpose and meaning of work at the top of their lists in terms of choosing an employer. The leadership narrative is essential to this. It reaffirms the organisation's purpose and should feed into all of its communications, be they recruitment materials, staff newsletters, press articles, training, and – for some organisations – through the product itself. This all begins with the CEO, as the way in which they communicate, and what they communicate, sets the tone for all others. The CEO's leadership narrative also plays an important part in modelling the culture and behaviours they intend to see demonstrated throughout the organisation.

Enabling improvement at scale. The leadership narrative should be clear about what success looks like through stories and anecdotes, as well as through customer feedback and ratings. It should celebrate achievements in line with the improvement and standards envisaged. The narrative should also place onus on issues such as collective commitment to organisational success, the importance of research and innovation, and the need for diligence and attention to detail. All of this is key to improvement at scale, and the more it features in the leadership narrative through stories, examples and anecdotes, the more it will influence and pervade the work.

Organisational sustainability and compliance. The leadership narrative determines the approach. It emphasises the importance of 'doing the right thing' and acting in the best interests of the organisation – particularly important in today's world. It will help guide leaders, senior managers, and staff, either directly or indirectly, in making both hard choices and strategic investments, because they will be clear on what the organisation values and prioritises.

Generating social and professional capital. As well as bringing staff along with you, the CEO also – more so than ever before – must bring people, groups and organisations along with them who could play a key part in generating social and professional capital or resources. In a world of austerity and complexity, such resource is essential to success, but people will only volunteer their time, energy and, indeed, money, if they relate to the organisation and its work. The CEO must use a compelling leadership narrative to forge the relationships and connections required.

Finally – communicate, communicate, communicate!

Alastair Campbell, the former Head of Communications for Tony Blair at 10 Downing Street, said that if he heard a groan from a group of reporters he knew his repetition was working. A CEO cannot overestimate the importance of communicating the leadership narrative. However, they should also seek to do so by leveraging a wide range of platforms and methods in which to share their message in multiple ways so that it remains engaging and as authentic as possible. In today's world, the good news is the mediums through which this can be achieved are expanding beyond the traditional staff briefings, internal newsletters, speeches and glossy brochures to online platforms such as Twitter, blogs and vlogs, and Skype.

Social media is being embraced by some CEOs, but not the majority. Recent research by UK public relations firm Ruder Finn, found CEOs of high performing are much more likely to be engaged in social media than lower performing ones. They have accounts with more posts and demonstrate higher levels of engagement with their followers. As the company's CEO, Kathy Bloomgarden was quoted as saying:

'We have reached a critical time in communications where a CEO's leadership style must evolve to stay current. As public figures, CEOs must find ways to leverage the power of social media as a means to bring their story to life and connect with customers, investors and other audiences, including employees. To be competitive, CEOs need to find their voice on social media, while carefully navigating the most important topics in the world today and staying relevant to their core business.'[19]

---

19. Ruder Finn. (2018) The Social CEO: How High Performing CEOs Use Social Media. Available at: www.ruderfinn.com/wp-content/uploads/2018/01/Social-CEO-Report.pdf

The research showed how successful CEOs also tended to provide more of a mix of industry-related posts then less successful CEOs, and were much more cautious to discuss politics or issues of controversy. It is also clear from my own conversations with CEOs, that those that use it now see it as a primary source of sector and wider intelligence and thought-leadership. It's also a great way of instigating valuable networking with people and organisations whose work aligns in some way with our own.

This all underlines the power of social media to bring about what I have discussed in this chapter – the need for CEOs to listen and engage; the need to find multiple opportunities for staying 'alive' to the world around them'; and the importance of sharing their leadership narrative in an engaging, authentic and inclusive way.

In a recent article on LinkedIn, Dr Josie Ahlquist of Florida State University listed her three big missteps that CEOs make on social media. At number one was 'a lack of presence' – such is the opportunity and all-pervading influence of it in the current day and age. The remaining two related to a lack of authenticity (having your account managed by someone else, perhaps a marketing person) and using the medium as a bulletin board (essentially 'telling' people what is happening, rather than engaging them in it). All themes we have touched on above.

We should certainly be cautious about relying too heavily on social media. Whilst it provides an exciting, time-efficient, and innovative platform for engagement, it is still no substitute for getting out and meeting people. It is also tempting to get sucked into debates and discussions that have little relevance or consequence in 'the real world'. It can make or break reputations within an instant, as CEOs respond immediately and fail to consider the consequences from the safety of their office or homes. The CEO who becomes remote or pompous through technology or otherwise does so at their peril.

Then, of course, there is traditional media – including local newspapers, television and radio – that will enter the CEO's orbit at some stage. It may be a crisis or a good news story that generates interest, but – either way – the CEO will be expected to provide a view or a response. Whether the story is positive or negative, the CEO must follow some golden rules here. First, they must relate the decision, action or development that is capturing interest to their leadership narrative. A CEO that can explain why something has happened, or (if an unforeseen or unfortunate event) the action they will take in response, and then relate it back to a well-established leadership narrative will stay true and retain confidence and engagement.

Some, when faced with the media, can either respond with fear or delusion, making statements that are reactive or incongruent. This is when things get messy. A CEO must pause for thought, take advice if necessary, think about how the event relates to the bigger picture – including the vision, values and strategy of the organisation – and then respond within that frame. If the issue comes down to a fundamental flaw or issue with the organisation's vision or overall direction, the chair should be involved in responding. Secondly, a CEO must not mislead, and should be as straight as possible with the media. It does nothing for a CEO to be unduly evasive or to be seen as dishonest later.

That said, and thirdly, it is important not to breach confidences and to protect those around us as much as possible. As we saw earlier, a CEO that shifts the blame or the passes the buck, especially to those they lead, will not retain followership for long. All in all, the traditional media remains a good vehicle for sharing the organisation's leadership narrative and for generating that, increasingly crucial, interest and engagement amongst communities in its work. A good CEO will recognise the power of that and not shy away from it.

In summary

Translating the vision into a compelling, authentic and inclusive leadership narrative is probably the most important aspect of a CEO's job. If it is done well, it can generate untold successes. By being close to those they serve and 'being alive' to the realities of the organisation and the world around them, a CEO not only shapes a leadership narrative that relates to people, they also shape a leadership narrative that is responsive to the needs of those they serve. This is almost a self-fulfilling leadership prophecy. The more we listen, the more we engage, the more we learn, the more we understand, the more we are respected and supported, and the better we lead.

The problem is that the title CEO is its own worst enemy. Too many CEOs consider themselves there to execute, not to listen or involve, or, indeed, to serve. Why should they need to do that? Surely, they have the power to do what they want when they want it, drawing on all their years of experience and knowledge? Yet, the best CEOs are 'alive' to the world around them, and so, therefore, are their leadership narratives and their strategy. That makes their leadership far more likely to gain traction and – in time – results. To step forward we must first step back and become the 'learner in chief'.

So, what are some of the key questions that CEOs can ask themselves in this area?

Questions for reflection

- Are you clear on the trust board's vision for the organisation? Do you know what their definition of success is so that you may confidently develop and pursue a leadership narrative that can engage, motivate and guide those at all levels of the organisation?

- Are you able to justify organisational growth/expansion/change in terms of the broader leadership narrative – rather than letting these 'means' define the organisation's 'ends'? What difference will growth or change make to your end users – the children and young people academy trusts serve?

- Are you investing sufficient time in reading the landscape and horizon scanning? Are you walking the halls and creating the space to listen to others and to read to inform strategic thinking?

Chapter 4

The all-important relationship between the CEO and the board

'The executive should understand what their board is there to do and wants to do and the ways in which it wants to do it, and then make it happen - all within the bounds of what is possible!'

- Vanni Treves

Vanni Treves is no stranger to the world of education, not least having successfully served as Chair of the National College for School Leadership for nearly a decade between 2004 and 2013. And, whilst his experience is largely drawn from beyond the schools' system in organisations such as Channel 4 and Equitable Life amongst others, he has long been a participant in the important dynamic that exists in so many organisations between the chair of the board and its executive leader. When I sit down to interview him, I consider myself to be in the presence of someone who has seen everything and done everything in relation to corporate governance. Yet the new and rather 'messy' world of academy trusts is one that clearly fascinates him.

'There are many parallels,' says Vanni, 'the first one being that the quality of your governing board – whatever the organisation – has an enormous bearing on the life and work, and therefore, success of the organisation. At the heart of this is the enormously important relationship between the chair and the executive leader. Every organisation's success rests on it, and it is something that must be given the investment of time, effort, and thought that it deserves.' Indeed, as we have seen so far in this book, the shared understanding between the CEO and board, and especially between the CEO and the chair, provides the cement between the four foundations of the CEO's role. As a recently retired academy trust CEO, Phil Crompton recently wrote in a Forum Strategy blog: 'If you don't think you can work with the chair then for heaven's sake don't take the job. It will torture you both – and the organisation.'

'The first thing to be very clear on', says Vanni, 'is that it is the board that has responsibility for setting the vision and direction for the organisation.' Indeed, Vanni believes that this understanding is at the foundation of a successful relationship between board and executive: 'The executive should understand what his/her board is there to do and wants to do and the ways in which it wants to do it, and then make it happen; all within the bounds of what is possible!' With such a fundamentally important task, we can see why it is so important that trust boards recruit and retain experienced and skilled trustees who have the right values and commitment for making a difference. Setting any organisation's vision and priorities is a major and influential undertaking to say the least.

However, the parallels do not end there. In the corporate world, as in the education world, the board has three or four major responsibilities, all of which must be understood and got right for the relationship to work. 'The board are there to do a number of things', says Vanni. 'They are there to set major priorities for the organisation; they are there to hold the executive leader to account; they are there to monitor and seek improvement of outcomes and ensure financial efficiency and compliance; and they have an important role in establishing an effective committee structure.' Indeed, Vanni's description closely resembles the core functions of governors of schools, which the current Department for Education governance handbook described as follows:

- Ensuring clarity of vision, ethos and strategic direction.
- Holding executive leaders to account for the performance of the organisation.
- Overseeing the financial performance of the organisation and making sure its money is well spent.[20]

Indeed, I would add – like Vanni – further aspects, including ensuring that governance is well structured and efficiently run, that it provides a supporting role to the CEO where necessary, and also – crucially – that it is self-improving.

For governing bodies this means that self and external review and talent audits are undertaken where necessary. The CEO can encourage such practice, but not compel it. A CEO has a vested interest in a board that performs as well as possible, and one that is made up of the right talents, skills and expertise to ensure they are supported and guided in their work. Compliance is also crucially important and we'll come to this in Chapter 7.

So what does an effective relationship between a board and its chief executive look like in practice? 'Clear and shared expectations are the starting point', says Vanni. 'Setting the priorities takes time. It requires clarity of thought and reflection on the part of the governing board, so that means creating the right conditions for this. I would recommend that governing boards spend at least one session a year away from their normal meeting environment to revisit and reflect on the vision and priorities and to make sure that they are as relevant and as purposeful as possible. Boards should find the space to consider the wider context, including the opportunities and challenges that their organisations face. They should also consider key trends, data, intelligence, and how all of this impacts on their core purpose, perhaps with some external input or provocation. That way they will be better equipped to provide clear direction in response. Where this is done well, and the direction is clearly communicated, it is much easier for the executive to know exactly which course they should be following and what the board expects them to deliver.'

---

20. Department for Education. (2017) *Governance handbook: For academies, multi-academy trusts and maintained schools.* Available at: www.gov.uk/government/uploads/system/uploads/attachment_data/file/582868/Governance_Handbook_-_January_2017.pdf

But what about strategy?

Clearly the board has responsibility for vision and overall organisational direction, but when it comes to strategy things are not always quite as clear. Is it the board's responsibility to determine strategy or the CEOs? Misunderstandings in this regard can lead to fundamental disagreements between boards and their CEOs, yet the answer is relatively simple. The board sets the direction through vision and high-level organisational objectives. The CEO, with reference to the board, determines how the organisation will get there.

On either side of this there are two extremes. On the one hand, boards that believe they should set strategy, which more or less demotes their CEO to the role of COO. And, on the other, a board that is completely 'hands off' in relation to strategy, and simply wait for the CEO to present it and then choose either to approve it or not.

In a 2018 article for Harvard Business Review, Roger L. Martin wrote: 'If the board feels it needs to do strategy for the company, it is prima facie evidence that it should fire the CEO. If a board that meets just a few days a year can do a better job of setting strategy than the CEO who is in the business 24/7, then the board as the wrong CEO.'[21]

Where the board and CEO relationship around strategy works, we see boards that provide their CEOs with clear direction and objectives – not least through performance management as we will see later in this chapter. The board will encourage the CEO to keep them informed on the development of strategy, providing advice and feedback at key junctures; but a strong board will resist the temptation to become involved in the 'nuts and bolts' of strategy development. A good CEO will seek to take ownership of formulating strategy, but they will also maximise the insight and feedback of the board every so often.

Martin recommends in the article *The Board's Role in Strategy* that CEOs take a three-step approach to engaging their boards on strategy:

1. 'Seek the board's input on the challenge that the board think the strategy should address.' CEO's need to be formulating a strategy that is focused on the outcomes the board wishes to achieve.

---

21. Martin, R, L. (28 December 2018) 'The Board's Role in Strategy'. (Harvard Business Review) Available at: https://hbr.org/2018/12/the-boards-role-in-strategy

2. 'In the middle of the process, the CEO should come back to the board with strategy possibilities – alternative approaches to deal with the challenges laid out in the first step.' This isn't about the CEO seeking ratification, but views on how the strategy can be improved and refined.

3. The CEO should present the desired strategy to the board, with what Martin describes as 'a fully baked strategy'. The board, by this stage, will have a clear idea of how and why the strategy has been developed in the way it has – not least because it is based on the direction it itself has set, and because it has been engaged and received opportunity to contribute insights and feedback. If the board and CEO are in a position where they fundamentally disagree on strategy at this stage, the relationship will break down.

All too often board/CEO relationships stumble on the question of 'who does strategy?' A CEO should have the confidence to assert their responsibility in this regard, but they should do so by taking care to involve their board, not least through seeking direction from the outset, and feedback and insight along the way. Ultimately, consensus must be agreed.

Accountability

Alongside this, accountability is a fundamental aspect of the relationship. 'It is the board's responsibility to hold the executive, and through him/her, other leaders to account. They must make sure they are doing the job as well as the board wishes them to do it, and support them to get better if they are not doing the job as well as they should be,' says Vanni. His view is that boards, whilst not 'meddling' or involving themselves in the operations of the organisation, should have a close eye on progress and be willing to provide the necessary support or challenge to leaders: 'Most leaders will need to reflect on their work and the progress they are making, and the board should give them the space to reflect, and to articulate what should happen next.'

Of course, this doesn't happen to the degree it should in every board. There are high profile organisations where the CEO seems to 'rule the roost'. Many will remember the former Chief Executive of Formula 1, Bernie Ecclestone, reflecting on occasion on the merits, as he perceived them, of dictatorial leadership[22] – a message that may have raised the eyebrows of some on the organisation's board. His unique style of leadership was considered to be dictatorial by some in the sport. Indeed, Ecclestone reportedly turned up to his first board meeting after the organisation was sold, but having been retained as Chief Executive, declaring that there was 'nothing special to report'.[23][24]

Such CEOs – perhaps through their sheer talent and force of personality – do exist, but it is essential to most organisations' long-term success and sustainability that a credible and strong board balances their influence. In the public sphere, far away from Ecclestone's world of fast cars, champagne and venture capitalists – where public money and public service delivery is at stake – the accountability is even more crucial. Yet, there have undoubtedly been CEOs in all sectors in the not so distant past that have 'ruled the roost' as it were, dominating their organisations and their boards for good or ill. Despite his success as CEO of Formula 1 (commercially at least), it was no particular surprise that Formula 1's new owners, Liberty Media, chose to replace Ecclestone as CEO of Formula 1 in 2017, replacing him with the much more corporate Chase Carey.

The days of 'dictator' or uncurtailed maverick CEOs, however talented they may be, are seemingly over. Professor Charles Elson, director of the Centre for Corporate Governance at the University of Delaware, recently wrote online: 'You need a strong independent board to counterweight a charismatic CEO otherwise… it can be a complete disaster.' Where there is a lack of accountability, he says that 'it renders the board meaningless, they become a cheering section.'[25]

Risk expert James Lam, President of James Lam & Associates, recently wrote about how boards could manage what he describes as 'white elephant'

22. The Guardian. (4 July 2009) 'Bernie Ecclestone says Hitler was a man who got things done'. Available at: www.theguardian.com/sport/2009/jul/04/bernie-ecclestone-interview-hitler-saddam
23. Bower, T. (2012) *No Angel: The Secret Life of Bernie Ecclestone*. London, England: Faber & Faber.
24. Eason, K. (2018) *Drive: The Men Who Made Formula One*. London, England: Hodder & Stoughton.
25. Easen, N. (23 October 2018) 'The role of the board in taming the CEO'. (Raconteur) Available at: www.raconteur.net/hr/board-ceo-governance

CEOs, those CEOs who are usually the genius behind a brand and have an all-pervading leadership influence, but have 'big issues that are extant but difficult to acknowledge and manage'. In this case, Lam was talking about the maverick technology tycoon Elon Musk, whose behaviour on social media led to him being temporarily removed from office in 2018. Lam says that 'white elephants are not acknowledged or dealt with on a timely and appropriate basis due to subjectivity'.[26] In this case, he advises, in order to address their behaviour, boards 'should invest in good governance, objective data and input from independent advisors, and crisis management plans. They should also invest in succession planning to reduce key person risks.'

How does this apply to multi-academy trusts?

There is no doubt that some of the early multi-academy trusts were led by people who could be described as 'mavericks' and even 'white elephant' CEOs. This was because these pioneering CEOs were given the job because they had a strong track record in school improvement, and were considered to be the best of the best. Like Bernie or Elon, they had seen their creation – successful school-to-school support partnerships – become corporate entities.

However, some of these new CEOs immediately recognised the scale of the transition and knew that both the size and the complexity of the organisations they were developing required them to have access to the support, guidance, and oversight of as talented a board as they could get their hands on. I remember the CEO of REAch2 Academy Trust, Sir Steve Lancashire, describing how the quality of his chair, Peter Little, was so fundamentally important to ensuring REAch2 became one of the leading and most impressive examples of academy trust growth and development. Despite his talent as a school improvement leader and the excellent leadership he demonstrated, he recognised that in order to be a great CEO he needed a great board that challenged him and advised him to the very highest standards possible. It was through his humility and self-awareness of his limitations that Sir Steve became a great CEO. Sir Steve and his team, including Cathie Paine and Dean Ashton, have

---

26. Levick, R. (7 November 2018) 'The Elon Musk Question: When Is 'Worth It' Really Worth It?' (Forbes) Available at: www.forbes.com/sites/richardlevick/2018/11/07/the-elon-musk-question-when-is-worth-it-really-worth-it/#4fa5101fbcb7

brought about positive change in dozens of school communities – often turning around generational failures. They are one of only a handful of trusts to operate at such a large scale that have managed to do this sustainably.

At the same time there have been trust boards that have simply fallen in line with the ambitions and views of their CEOs. These boards have 'nodded through' rapid expansions pursued by egotistical CEOs, failed to challenge failures in schools and school improvement where they evidently existed, and – in the worst cases – overseen the awarding of contracts to private companies and organisations linked to the CEO. These examples are well known and have received widespread media attention. What is clear is that none of them would have happened were it not for the ego or arrogance of an unrestrained CEO, operating with a board that failed to challenge them on the most basic and fundamental issues. What is almost certainly lost in all of these cases is the all-important sense of accountability and responsibility to the end-users (for MATs, their children, young people and communities), which is always generated and secured by good governance.

In less extreme cases we have lonely CEOs, who do not have the board of talented people embraced by Sir Steve and are in the rather strange position of having to lead their recruitment. This is a dangerous position for any CEO to be in, and it is up to the members of the trust, and the chair, to appoint a board of the highest calibre. The CEO's role should simply be to embrace the accountability and the guidance for all it is worth. This is a policy issue that reflects government's sheer failure in recent years to devise initiatives and incentives to ensure the most talented and experienced people possible are putting themselves forward for these positions. Simply put, if a CEO does not feel they have the board they deserve, they need to look at changing organisation – however attached they are to the one they are currently working in. Only then will the powers that be realise that more work needs to be done.

The CEO's report

Formal communication lines – in particular, board papers – are also vitally important to the functioning of the board and the success of the relationship between it and the executive. Vanni is clear that these should be put together by the executive, with a summary of the key contents of all the board papers forming a document at the front. 'The executive's report is the most important document – it should readily highlight key issues of concern to the executive, in a what's good, what's bad and what I'm working on format, so that this is clear and upfront.'

Vanni believes that a lot of trouble should be taken with the composition of board papers, so that the chair and trustees can properly discharge their responsibilities, knowing they have the information they need in a clear format. Informal communication lines are also important, and should be encouraged, but the executive should always keep the chair informed of his/her dealings with other board members.

The CEO's report is a crucial mechanism in ensuring a strong and effective relationship with the trust board. The report should present information to the level and standard required, and provide the basis for constructive, strategic discussion and decision-making.

A key question that CEO's often ask me is: 'what does a good CEO report look like?' There are a number of important elements, but the starting point is this: 'what does your board want and need to know?' A conversation with the chair, and potentially the board as a whole, is a very important starting point. The CEO MUST endeavour to meet their requirements in terms of the level and scope of information provided.

That considered, the CEO's report should be no more than three sides (although it may have appendices if appropriate) and be sufficiently high level and strategic in nature. Vanni's advice is for the CEO's report to tell the board three things:

- What's going well.
- What's not going well – key risks and strategic challenges.
- What I'm actively working on/prioritising.

(I would also add 'what I currently need from you as a board').

That seems like a reasonable structure to adopt, ensuring all the time that the report remains strategic and doesn't present extensive operational details (this should, if necessary, be left for another, more extensive agenda item and paper). The National Governance Association also provide some useful guidance in their publication 'Welcome to a Multi-Academy Trust', which states that, as far as trustees are concerned: 'the report should give you enough information to carry out your role, but not weigh you down with so much information that it is impossible to determine the important from the merely interesting.'

Unfortunately, I have seen examples where the CEO's report is a comprehensive 'deep dive' into the issues and developments across every facet of the organisation. That is simply not how a CEO should be reporting to their board. It clouds strategic discussion and can often feel like a CEO needing therapy or counselling, rather than looking for a steer and some high-level challenge.

The CEO report can also sometimes take a back seat where, for example, the CEO and chair have a good working relationship, meeting and speaking regularly and keeping one another informed. Whilst it is good that CEOs and chairs maintain good and active lines of communication, the problem comes when the CEO and chair consider this to be a substitute for the CEO report. In such a case, the wider board may find itself less well appraised of the organisation's progress (or lack of), and therefore less able to provide challenge and support to the executive.

Finally, it is extremely important that the CEO's report is not confused with performance management. It is essential that the CEO feels confident in reporting key developments, including challenges, relating to the organisation and that they do so without incurring a sense of being under cross-examination of their own performance. The report should encourage constructive challenge, but this distinction is of utmost importance.

Performance management of the CEO

It is more often the case that good CEOs accept – and indeed, encourage – accountability from their board. They know that accountability is essential to transparency, to generating advice and support where necessary, and to their own improvement.

Much of this rests on a CEO receiving a high standard of appraisal, which provides a careful blend of support and challenge to the executive leader. 'Being a CEO or executive leader can be a lonely business', says

Vanni, 'and it is the job of the board to help the CEO do as good a job as they can. A well-run appraisal that ties into the organisational vision and priorities, and that sufficiently 'stretches' the executive, whilst also putting in place the necessary professional development and support alongside it, is a really crucial means of keeping the leader and organisation on track. Boards can also ensure that the executive leader is receiving mentoring, as well as constructive feedback and challenge through 360 degree reviews, helping them to be more reflective on how their leadership is contributing to the organisation's culture and progress.'

A CEO must be given the chance to have an input on their targets and objectives, without heavily influencing these or having any final say on what they should be. A CEO should be encouraged to enter into dialogue about how their performance objectives and their opportunities for professional development, relate sufficiently to the organisation's vision and strategic priorities.

What a CEO should expect from performance management

Step 1: At the beginning of the year, and following the conclusion of the previous year's end-of-year appraisal, the board (led by the chair and another trustee/board member) should provide the CEO with some draft objectives and development priorities. The board should enter into dialogue with the CEO on these, and the CEO should have the opportunity to review and feedback on them.

Step 2: The board will make the final call on the objectives and development priorities for the year ahead. These should be carefully aligned with organisational vision and strategic priorities. They should be SMART in nature. The CEO's development needs should also be reflected and prioritised.

Step 3: The CEO should expect that the objectives and targets rest on a range of objective sources of data and intelligence, which can be triangulated to ensure an accurate overall picture of the CEO's performance over a given period.

Step 4: The CEO should gain the opportunity at least through a mid-year review and before the year-end review to provide their view on how well they have performed, and whether they feel they have 'exceeded', 'met', 'partly met' or 'not met' their objectives.

Step 5: The CEO should expect the board to provide detailed feedback on their performance both at mid-year review and at the end of year review, having already had the opportunity to provide their own perspective beforehand.

Step 6: The CEO should expect the process to include a guarantee of opportunities to access high quality professional development, including mentoring.

I would also recommend that the performance management process carefully reflects the framework in this book, which provides a good structure for these purposes. As such, a board can ensure that the full-breadth of the CEO role and its key 'pillars' are captured both in terms of reviewing performance and providing professional development opportunities.

Clear demarcation of responsibilities

'It's particularly important that there are clear demarcation lines between the chair and the executive', says Vanni. 'In many cases it can be impossible to prescribe or determine this formally for all cases because it is impossible to anticipate every situation and circumstance. However, it is important that executives and the board maintain communication so that there is no stepping on toes.' Again, some of this depends on high quality induction, for both the chair and executives, so that there is a clear understanding of the separation of roles and responsibilities from the outset.

No surprises!

Finally, I ask Vanni what he considers to be the most frequent causes of trouble between a board and its executive. 'Surprises. It is important that any concerns or risks should be communicated as soon as possible. The last thing a board wants is to be reactive because it hasn't received the necessary information early enough. It undermines the good governance of the organisation and, of course, the relationship between the board and the executive leader.' Other frequently cited issues range from disagreements on vision and strategy, where the board and the executive don't agree on the overall strategy for the organisation, through to poor board/chairman/executive chemistry. If these relationships are not sound, it will be obvious to other members of the board and other staff so action will need to be taken by those concerned to resolve any issues. If they can't be resolved then either the executive or the chair could be asked to leave, and Vanni suggested it would almost always be the executive that stays, if they are strong, performing well and have the support of the wider board. Likewise, a weak board can be a major source of problems. It is very demotivating for the executive leader if board members lack commitment, don't attend meetings, haven't read the papers and don't collaborate. Vanni said he couldn't emphasise enough the importance of taking the time to ensure schools and trusts recruit the best boards possible for their organisations. Vanni ends with this:

'Where you see successful organisations, you will almost always see a strong relationship between the chair and executive that is defined by the necessary investment of time, effort and good quality of communication. The board and the executive have a responsibility to one another, and respecting that and acting upon it is essential to everyone's success. In schools it is, ultimately, the children and young people who will benefit, and that is why everyone, not least governing board members, turn up to do the job they do. That's extremely rewarding.'

Questions for reflection

- Do you feel that your relationship with the board is as strong, open and constructive as it can be? Are you both clear on lines of demarcation and respective roles in relation to vision and strategy development?
- Is your performance management delivered in a way that is clearly linked to organisational vision and strategy? Does it include access to relevant professional development and support?
- Are you confident in your strategic reporting to the board? Is strategic reporting accessible, relevant and a helpful platform

for the necessary conversations and decisions that 'need to be had' at board level?

- Is there overlap between executive leadership and local governing body responsibilities? How can you and the chair seek to ensure separation and better clarity around responsibilities and reporting?

Chapter 5

Chief Talent Officer
and Culture Maker

'None of us, including me, ever do great things.
But we can all do small things, with great love,
and together we can do something wonderful.'

– Mother Teresa

If there is one key message I hope to come from this book, it is this –
humility is a powerful trait within a modern CEO. The sheer complexity,
pace of change, and the limitations of 'the individual' in today's world all
means that the great CEOs today are facilitators of success. A CEO is not
a one man or woman hurricane of change. They are, as the title suggests,
a 'chief', which implies that central to the work is that of the band of
people around them.

In that vein, I wish to define what we mean by 'chief', and I believe it
is this: part 'Chief Talent Officer' and part 'Chief Decision Maker'. To
be the best Chief Decision Maker one can be, I strongly believe that a
modern CEO needs to be the best Chief Talent Officer they can be. It is
the role of Chief Talent Officer and 'Culture Maker' that I wish to cover
in this chapter.

For every CEO, both building the right team around you and building the capacity of the wider organisation to deliver is a prerequisite to success. As Chief Talent Officer, the CEO must constantly be working to create an environment that attracts great people and then enables them to flourish. With talented, motivated, and committed staff on board at all levels, the job of the CEO becomes far easier and the organisation's path to success, more assured. As Joe Trammell, author of *The CEO Tightrope*, writes:

'I have always felt that I should attribute the majority of my success to my efforts to get the right people in the right positions. For me, it has been the most important task, because I believe that all the strategy in the world cannot make up for a lack of capabilities.'

It begins with you (and then your team)

The importance of the quality of the CEO's immediate team cannot be underestimated. As with Lincoln's 'team of rivals', the effective CEO will aim to recruit a 'team of experts'; people who are better and more expert than they are. Like Lincoln, the CEO will sufficiently supress ego and the need to be seen as the 'master of the universe' in order to attract a team of people who are better than they are.

'The number one job of a leader is to bring on board the right people.' – Sir John Jones[27]

Indeed, striving to bring on board a group of people from whom they can seek advice, support, and challenge, and whom they can trust to deliver, can make or break a CEO's tenure. Recent research by Harvard Business Review found that 'any weakness in this group (the senior leadership team) significantly reduces the CEOs' effectiveness.'[28] CEOs need top senior teams. But how do they do they achieve this? First of all, they must wholly subscribe to the enormous importance of attracting, recruiting and retaining a high-quality senior team.

A CEO I know and admire was recently award a CBE for service to education. When I wrote to him to congratulate him on his honour, the reply I received was simple and to the point: 'I am merely standing on

---

27. Jones, J. (2018) *Inspiring Leaders Annual Conference*. [Speech] 30 November.
28. Porter, M & Nohria, N. (2018) 'How CEOs Manage Time'. (Harvard Business Review) Available at: https://hbr.org/2018/07/the-leaders-calendar

the shoulders of giants'. My response to his message was to highlight how this attitude was surely the reason he had achieved such success and subsequent recognition.

Yet we do live in a society that hails the hero leader, attaching every success (and indeed, every failure), to the influence of the individual at the top. This could be considered by some to be a very old-fashioned view, but it also speaks to part of the human psyche that it is very hard to undo, and every CEO must be aware of it. People look to individuals rather than teams as figureheads of movements – including organisations. If we consider great leaders such as Mandela, Mother Theresa, and indeed Lincoln, we know that despite being leaders of a movement that involved the leadership of many people, they are personally associated with that movement to the detriment of others. Ask a group of people 'who is Neil Armstrong?' and you will get a room full of raised hands. Ask the same group of people who Michael Collins is, and you will get one or two hands at most. Michael Collins stayed in orbit in Apollo 14 whilst Neil and Buzz Aldrin landed on the moon.

The CEO must recognise this. They must be mindful that – as my friend, Steve Munby often says – they 'wear the mantle of leadership'. Their every move and message is scrutinised by those that follow them. They must wear that mantle with care, and ensure that they involve, support, empower and recognise those around them who, whilst more junior than them within the organisation, are also likely to be more expert and more informed in their areas of specialism and knowledge.

The CEO is not merely the boss of those other leaders, they are also the servant of them. That is a very fine balance to manage. A recent article by Insead Knowledge stated that: 'Knowledge workers need both headroom and elbowroom to be productive. Good CEOs create this autonomy by giving their people freedom to work the way they want and make their own decisions. Effective CEOs should make as few decisions as possible, giving the opportunity instead to other people in the organisation.'[29] This begins with the CEO's senior team.

29. Shekshnia, S & Kravchenko, K. (9 May 2018) 'CEOs Should Be Chief Enablement Officers'. (INSEAD Knowledge.) Available at: https://knowledge.insead.edu/leadership-organisations/ceos-should-be-chief-enablement-officers-9056

My friend and colleague David Strudley, a long time CEO with enormous experience of leading within 'high stakes' organisations, such as the army and children's hospices, articulates this extremely well. 'I really do believe that the thing that marks out the success of leadership is that when you feel the sense of 'us', not 'you and I'.... there is a balance of respect, and the ability to provide sufficiently informed challenge as CEO. A team should feel well supported and well directed by the CEO. The worst thing is not to care.'

Now some CEOs, I'm afraid, miss the point here completely – particularly 'the respect' aspect. They grab the limelight, they take credit for success, and they believe that their name is the organisation's greatest asset. Worst still, they try to hide behind others when failure hits. Have you ever met a leader like that? I have, and they're not motivating to work for. The problem with these CEOs, to coin another of Steve Munby's phrases, is that they have ended up 'drinking their own bathwater'. People see this and, frankly, they do not wish to work for these people. This is a key undoing of a CEO: losing their ability to recruit and retain a talented team of people around them. Anyone who has witnessed the unravelling and rapid turnover of staff in the White House over the last two years, for example, can see how the ego-driven leader can have this effect. Talented people just don't stick around.

Before they can build or rebuild the senior team or the wider capacity of the organisation so that it is a 'hot house' of talent, a CEO must therefore seek to establish themselves, personally, as an 'employer of choice'. Be under no illusions, this is about the CEO being an employer of choice in the first instance, then the organisation; such is the CEO's influence in setting the organisational 'temperature'. A senior team will only work with a CEO who they enjoy working for and feel a commitment to, and it is then for the senior team to help them deliver that employer of choice culture.

A CEO's reputation as a team player, as someone who empowers and supports others, goes before them. As David Strudley says: 'we get the leaders and the team we deserve.'

Senior team culture is important, and once the right people are in place, an effective CEO will invest time in developing a team that demonstrates disciplined listening, openness to feedback, and a commitment to leaving egos at the door. They will also invest time in helping each member of the team to see their role in delivering upon the vision and shaping the strategy. None of this is time wasted for the effective CEO who will dedicate themselves to both coaching and managing their senior teams well. As recent research by the Boston Consulting Group found:

'Leaders cannot simply set the broad vision for a transformation and then delegate its execution. Instead, they must show directive leadership, setting the ambition, articulating strategic priorities, and holding management accountable for results. At the same time, they need to be inclusive, involving their teams early on, fostering collaboration, soliciting honest feedback, and empowering teams to define and implement specific initiatives. Striking this balance can be difficult.'[30]

The analogy of the Grand Prix pit crew

One of the best examples of teamwork you will ever see is the work of a Formula 1 pit crew during a Grand Prix pit stop. Indeed, the work of an excellent pit crew can provide many lessons for the senior team of an organisation. Motor racing is often perceived as a sport of 'heroes', with racing drivers with big egos and bank balances driving around alone in their cars chasing glory and standing aloft on a podium, enjoying all the spoils of victory. Yet behind any successful grand prix driver is their team, often running into many hundreds of people, from engineers and aerodynamicists, to race strategists, physiotherapists, and caterers. Grand Prix races are often won by a handful of seconds, and a crucial part in gaining the advantage during a 200 mile race is at the 'pit stop', where the car's tyres (and sometimes settings) are changed mid race by a crew of around 20 mechanics.

Pit stops are an awe-inspiring example of teamwork to witness. The record time in which a car has had all four tyres changed is 1.9 seconds! Yet, within those 1.9 seconds, a team of people performs a set of highly choreographed, specialist functions. Each one needs to be discharged in the right order, by the right person, and to inform a very important decision: when the car

---

30. Burkner, H, P, Faeste, L, Hemerling, J, Lyusina, Y & Reeves, M. (7 November 2017) 'The Transformations That Work – and Why'. (BCG) Available at: www.bcg.com/publications/2017/transformations-people-organization-that-work-why.aspx

is ready to leave the pit area and return to the racetrack. I say it again: all within 1.9 seconds (if you are truly on the button)!

The pit crew must do a number of things:

- The driver must enter the pit area at approximately 50mph and stop precisely so that each wheel is aligned with a small team of people who will service the car. If the car is a few centimetres out of position, the crew will need to physically move themselves and their equipment. This in itself will take at least a couple of seconds.
- One person within the crew on each of the car's four corners will use a 'wheel gun' to remove the wheel nut so that the wheel comes off rapidly. Engaging the gun as soon as the wheel stops and so that the gun immediately connects with the nut is crucial. Any delay could lose the race.
- Immediately it is another person's job to take off the wheel at exactly the moment the wheel nut is disengaged. Tyres are heavy, cumbersome (and extremely hot!) objects to remove. They must lift the tyre accurately and remove themselves from the immediate scene as soon as possible, so as not to hinder the other members of the team.
- A third person will place the new wheel onto the car, accurately and smoothly (remember these are heavy objects), with each of the new tyres having already been brought up to 'race track' temperature (using a heated blanket) by a dedicated mechanic in the garage.
- Finally the wheel gun operator is now ready to secure the wheel nut of the new wheel. This, again, must be done at precisely the moment the wheel is placed onto the car. The operator does not want to drop the wheel nut or cross-thread it when securing the wheel as this could be the difference between winning the Grand Prix and finishing off the podium. A team of hundreds of people are depending on you.
- Once the nut of the new wheel and tyre is secured, the wheel gun operator will raise his hand.

At the same time other members of the crew will be making adjustments to the car's aerodynamic settings (based on feedback from the driver or the telemetry being sent back to the garage). These individual mechanics are specialists in the aerodynamic settings of the car and will know exactly what to do to modify and enhance aerodynamic performance – but they must, like those changing the tyres, make these alterations quickly and precisely.

Finally, the car is up 'on the jacks' throughout the pit stop. The jack operators at the front and rear of the car must lift the jacks as soon as the driver parks the car in the appropriate space. Once the wheels have been serviced and the aerodynamic changes have been made, each operator will raise their hands. The rear jack will go down, and the front jack operator will check for a full group of raised hands amongst all members of the crew whilst also having an eye to make sure that there is a clear track for the car to return to. Any misjudgment in this regard will lead to the car having to stop for further repairs or, even worse, being involved in an accident with another car on exiting the pit area.

The pit crew are very much like a CEO's senior leadership team. The CEO (the driver) must create the right conditions – they must ensure the car is well placed for people to do their jobs, they must provide feedback about the car via radio throughout the race to allow their team to consider the right decisions to make regarding the aerodynamic set up, and they must have faith in their crew so that when they take the decision (to put the accelerator down) they will exit the pit lane with all four wheels secured and without the risk of accident. Whilst the drivers' rear view mirrors are full of their team members when they are parked (very briefly) in the pits, they must be alert when taking the decision to leave as to whether that decision is the right one. Sometimes, despite the best judgment of the team around them, they must apply the brakes!

At the end of the race, if successful, the driver, like the CEO, will be hailed as a success. The press, the crowd, and the team will gather round them. The great Grand Prix driver will always remember to thank and recognise their team. They know that they cannot get out of the car to change their wheels and the aerodynamic settings of the car, or, indeed, to operate the jacks and advise on when the circumstances are ready and safe for leaving the pit area.

Former Grand Prix driver David Coulthard is a man who has won and lost international Grand Prix races based on the efficiency of his pit crew. He recognises the importance of the sense of a team of experts, all contributing to 'his' success, and with that was also very mindful of his role in setting the temperature. In his book, *The Winning Formula*, he says:

'The team is very tight knit, there is a strong sense of interdependence; we work together, we lose together, and be safe together. You have to ask yourself; if you'd been rude to that pit crew the week before, are you sure they will be 100% committed to your tyre change? Most will likely still be committed, because they can separate their emotions and deliver their job, but what if there is one guy who did take offence, who remembered that you paid him no attention or respect a few days ago at the factory, maybe he is even thinking about that as you pit… that's how mistakes can be made or lost. In a world where margins are measured in tenths of a second or less, anything other than full commitment and focus will not give you the win.'

The importance of the driver or CEO's role in 'respecting' their team, and the skills, expertise and contribution that each person makes, is crucial; it builds, as Coulthard and David Strudley say, a sense of 'us', and also a culture of professional trust and responsibility that make success a reality in what is a complex and interdependent world. No racing driver can change their wheels and settings in two seconds and then go on to win, and no CEO can drive improvement and success in their own organisation, without this same 'team culture', where all talents are respected, empowered and trusted.

How does this apply to multi-academy trusts?

Crucial to all MAT CEOs are those senior school improvement leaders (those with NLE or LLE level experience) who can drive improvement and ensure educational standards at scale, without the day-to-day involvement of the CEO. It is impossible for a CEO to ensure the standards in every school, and that improvement is taking place on a day-to-day or even week-to-week basis. The same applies to the other key facets of the organisation led by people such as the Chief Operating Officer, HR and IT leaders, and those people who are responsible for ensuring that sites and premises are safe and inspiring places to work and learn.

However, in my experience, the recruitment of a highly effective school improvement leader is a big test of academy trust CEOs. The CEO must let go of the day-to-day leadership responsibility in this regard; despite the fact many have built up their professional credibility and reputation by leading school improvement so well. Letting go of – without taking ones eyes off – this work is a big test of whether the CEO has made the leap from lead professional to corporate leader. They must set the right tone in empowering their school improvement leads to make plans and key judgments and decisions without their involvement, despite their many years of experience. As we see in Chapter 6, the CEO must look to the robust and real time data and intelligence to ensure they still have a handle on the impact of improvement, without becoming consumed by operational leadership matters.

Many CEOs, in my experience, are delighted to let go the operations of financial leadership, but they must always remain strategic and 'eyes on' in this regard. They may be ready and willing to leave leadership of this work to others, but they must ensure they are an integrated part of the team, contributing to strategy and operations whenever necessary. The CEO must also be ready to apply the brakes or change direction in regard to all facets of the organisation's work!

The role of intuition

In concluding the analogy, it is worth reflecting on the moment of intuition just a little more – the moment when the CEO makes the call 'to leave the pits or apply the brakes'. This is essentially what the CEO is paid for: to make the calls and to take the risks. On the desk in my office I have a sculpture of a crouched and solitary figure, poised on the edge of precipice and contemplating making the leap. This is the moment, after all the discussion is had and advice is taken, where it all comes down to intuition, or 'gut'. The moment when leadership truly happens and decisions are finally made for good or ill.

As an entrepreneur and business owner, I consider this moment to be 'the starkest' aspect of leadership – the final call. Do I commit our resources to this project? Do I make a public commitment to take this course of action? Am I content to make this big appointment? Ultimately, the decision is ours and sometimes decisions can be so strategically profound that, in the long run, they can make or break our leadership and, potentially, our organisation's success and future. There is no getting away from these moments, they are often defining and every leader with ultimate decision-making responsibility for the organisation will experience them at some point, perhaps on a regular basis.

Ultimately, in these moments, it comes down to our intuition as leaders. Spinoza, the 17th century philosopher, called intuition a 'superior way of knowing ultimate truth without the use of prior knowledge or reason'. No one can completely guarantee or predict the outcome of a course of action. Our intuition is certainly no guarantee of success. Yet, in the end, our intuition often plays a central role in making that final call. Leaders from Steve Jobs and Oprah Winfrey, to Bill Gates and Richard Branson are all widely quoted on its central role in their success. Indeed, some argue – including themselves – that it has been a central tenet to their success. One could also argue that intuition has let some of these people down more than once on the road to their success.

In an article for Harvard Business Review, Modesto A. Maidique, President Emeritus and Executive Director of the Center for Leadership at Florida International University in Miami, outlined the findings from his interviews with 20 leading CEOs about the best and worst decisions they had made during their careers. For the most part, the CEOs considered their decisions – both good and bad – to ultimately have been made through 'gut'. However, Maidique also found that where the CEOs had made a good 'gut' decision, this was often in a realm that related closely to their area of professional expertise and experience. Where they made bad 'gut' decisions, these were often outside the realm of their experience and expertise.

Maidique concluded that 'at its best, the key to effective, intuitive decisions is best conveyed in two wise sayings: 'know your business' and 'know yourself.' The sweet spot for business decisions is when both domain knowledge and self knowledge are high; when you have the knowledge to shrewdly interpret the facts and the wisdom to steer clear of the biases and destructive emotions that can hinder success.'[31]

What we can say is that intuition can be fostered – if not generated – by a number of key elements. We can bolster our intuition by ensuring we stay attuned to our surroundings; maintaining contextual wisdom and giving ourselves the time to reflect and think, as is covered in Chapter 3; putting ourselves in a position where we are informed, advised and challenged by expert and values-driven people, including our board, who can highlight our biases or lack of knowledge; and, finally, by maintaining a careful balance of humility and self-confidence drawn from our own experience as leaders and as people. After that, we are alone, and we must decide whether our intuition is sufficiently bolstered.

One thing is certain: a good CEO cannot ignore the importance of intuition.

Building the team around you

Attracting the most capable candidates to our teams is essential to the CEO's and the organisation's success, yet it can often be a rushed process as CEOs seek to recruit anyone of sufficient calibre in order to fulfil their growth plans. This is a big mistake. Indeed, recent analysis by Harvard Business Review found that the number one regret of CEOs after they had been in office awhile was 'not setting high-enough standards in selecting direct reports'.[32] Savvy CEOs in both growing and established organisations anticipate this, and are always on the look out for these high potential senior leaders.

How do they do this? They network intensely and cultivate relationships with people who may, one day, be looking to move. I know of one CEO who keeps a careful directory of people she has met through her networking and meetings who really impress her. She doesn't just leave it there. She makes sure to send them a Christmas card each year, to send

---

31. Maidique, M, A. (13 April 2011) 'Intuition Isn't Just about Trusting your Gut'. (Harvard Business Review) Available at: https://hbr.org/2011/04/intuition-good-bad-or-indiffer
32. Porter, M & Nohria, N. (2018) 'How CEOs Manage Time'. (Harvard Business Review) Available at: https://hbr.org/2018/07/the-leaders-calendar

a 'keeping in touch' email every six months or so to see how they are getting on, and, if they are really impressive, to invite them to visit her organisation and her meet her team and share ideas. That is long-term headhunting. The Chief Talent Officer CEO doesn't wait until a senior job turns up to start, but when it does she rarely has to start from scratch by delegating such an important task to an expensive headhunting company that cannot easily connect in with the culture, vision and values of the organisation.

Alongside this, CEOs also recognise their role in becoming an employer of choice. They recognise the innate value of a shaping a talent-powered culture over time, and then to make sure to develop and promote their organisations as employers of choice; places where people aspire to work. An integral part of this is having internal leadership development programmes that help promote talented people who are committed to the vision and values of the organisation into senior leadership roles over time.

Taking hard decisions: When people aren't right

The job of CEO is not simply about keeping people motivated, inspired, engaged and developed. Sometimes it is about addressing underperformance and, in some cases, moving people on.

A CEO cannot compromise a strong and effective team by tolerating someone whose performance or values simply falls short.

In his book, *Winners*, Alastair Campbell describes one of the best examples of a leader doing just this. President Truman's team of talent included the war hero General Douglas MacArthur, a man who had been Supreme Commander Southwest Pacific Area, in World War II. MacArthur had been a supreme war leader, defending and retaking the Philippines and accepting the Japanese surrender. MacArthur took a very different view to Truman on Korea. Whilst Truman wanted to limit military intervention, MacArthur wanted to invade China and use nuclear weapons to break down communism. MacArthur's views were not aligned with government policy and Truman asked him to stop repeating them, but he did not. In April 1951, Truman removed MacArthur from his command. Campbell includes a quote from Truman's biography, where he explains why he removed MacArthur:

'I fired him because he wouldn't respect the authority of the President. I didn't fire him because he was a dumb son of a bitch, although he was, but that's not against the laws for generals. If it was, half to three-quarters of them would be in jail [...]. I'm afraid he wasn't right in the head. And there was never anyone around to keep him in line. He didn't have anyone on his staff who wasn't an ass kisser [...]. The only thing I learned out of the whole MacArthur deal is that when you feel there's something you have to do and you know in your gut you have to do it, the sooner you get it over with, the better everybody is.'

As we have seen, CEOs rely on intuition in order to take decisions based on the advice of their teams; in some cases they rely on their team wholly. If they cannot trust a team member – either because they are incompetent or not aligned with the values of the organisation – this presents a major risk.

Kate Lester, CEO of Diamond Logistics, one of the one hundred fastest growing companies in the UK in 2018, says this: 'the thought of getting rid of a resource far outweighs the ramifications of doing so. And you have no idea how much additional time, energy, and management these resources are actually taking up [...]. Don't accept incompetence. It damages your team, your clients and your progress.'[33] Kate argues that some CEOs risk seeing other people as irreplaceable, not least because a team of experts, competent or otherwise, surrounds them. That should not be a barrier, and CEOs must confront the difficult issue of a team member who is either not performing or not conducive to the values, culture and direction of the organisation. Your team members will also be senior leaders in their own right, so this is about more than the job they do; it is about the leadership they model.

Addressing underperformance and, if necessary, 'letting people go' as a CEO has to be done with care. That is why every CEO invests in good performance management of staff; not only to ensure people are 'on track' and accountable (as well as supported) to deliver against their remit, but also to ensure that challenges and deviations from the standards and

---

33. Lester, K. (2014) *Stop Reading Self Help Books*. Kate Lester.

values of the team are identified and – if possible – addressed. If not, good performance management allows us to make hard decisions fairly and transparently, where they need to be made. There is a lot of talk currently about the need to ditch the term performance management and to move to 'performance development'. I don't buy this. You can care for your team and love your team, whilst also ensuring accountability. The stakes are too high when it comes to the CEO's team, and their dependency on that team, not to have this in place.

Forging a talent-powered culture

With a strong senior leadership team in place, a CEO can go about cementing the culture, key to which is maximising the talents and contributions of its people. As recent research by Egon Zehnder underlined the fact that 'the CEO and the leadership set the tone of a company's culture. It has been said that an organisation cannot perform at a higher level than its leadership's consciousness.'[34] It is the CEO as employer of choice, supported by a team of talented experts who share the same values and mindset, which can then go about shaping a culture for success.

The best CEOs also see it as their responsibility to oversee that there is a pipeline of talented staff and that it holds onto the best people. They make sure that the organisation invests in their learning, growth and wellbeing to secure retention. They keep a careful handle on the organisation's strategy for becoming an 'employer of choice' and constantly have reference to the views and feedback of their staff in taking it forward. A good CEO will ensure they have the intelligence to understand how their staff are feeling and what the major barriers are that they face. After all, the reputation of the organisation as an employer will always stem from its staff.

Indeed, being an employer of choice and capturing talent for the organisation has never been higher up the radar of a CEO. KPMG's UK CEO Outlook 2017[35] found that recruitment will be a CEOs top area of investment over the next three years, with 77% saying they will invest highly in people. This is fundamentally a strategic issue for the CEO, devised in partnership with

---

34. EgonZehnder. (2018) 'The CEO: A personal reflection'. Available at: https://ceostudy.egonzehnder.com/The-CEO-report-Egon-Zehnder.pdf
35. KPMG. (2017) 'UK CEO Outlook 2017'. Available at: https://home.kpmg/content/dam/kpmg/uk/pdf/2017/06/uk-ceo-outlook-2017.pdf

their HR directors and senior team, which must then translate into delivery. It is strategic, not least because the expectations of employees and the very nature of the employment market is changing rapidly. This is partly driven by those key disruptors I mentioned earlier, and will come back to again, austerity, technology and the complexity of 'the work'.

So what do those changes look like? What is it that CEOs need to be 'alive to' in terms of employee expectations and needs? The first thing is a need to look forwards, to ensure that employment models and conditions are adapting to the new generation of workers, and that organisations are not experiencing workplace culture inertia. A CEO should very much have this on their radar, as should their board, as the employer.

A recent survey by Deloitte showed that the key things those under 35 are looking for in their work are sense of purpose; ability to make use of their skills; involvement in a variety of experiences; access to professional development; and aligned values. However, there are some more specific issues at play currently. In a recent interview with Inspiring Leaders magazine, Mandy Coalter, a thought-leader and HR practitioner working in the education sector, stated that 'people increasingly want the option to work more flexibly. Due to technology, flexible working has become more common, and this has led to a change in expectations. People want the option to work flexibly so that they have increased control over their schedule and can make work fit around other commitments.' This is a trend that is being taken very seriously by employers and organisations across the wider economy.

The research around the expectations of Generation Z employees is now only beginning to emerge, and for every CEO it should be treated like gold dust. This kind of information is critical to organisations and CEOs who are future-proofing their talent pipelines and looking to meet the expectations of a new generation of employees. Indeed, the same KPMG survey of CEOs referred to above, found a clear trend amongst CEOs in terms of 'placing more emphasis on the millennial generation, and the different way in which they will impact on (and interact with) the workplace.'

Secondly, a good CEO will ensure that they have intelligence and knowledge about their employees' perceptions of work. This should include what their needs are, what the barriers they face are, and what they enjoy most and least about working for the organisation. Employee perceptions should be regularly monitored and analysed to inform organisational strategy. The CEO should be regularly reporting to their board on these issues, and, in my view, be accountable to their board for whether they are fostering an 'employer of choice' culture.

Thirdly, a CEO should be supporting and holding their own senior team to account for their contributions and leadership of the employer of choice culture. Like the CEO themselves, their senior team should be accountable for the recruitment and retention of the best staff, and how those staff are being developed, where appropriate, for leadership roles within the organisation.

Shaping the organisation's reputation as an employer of choice

So what can a CEO do to establish that reputation as an employee of choice? First of all, they can establish that sense of purpose, communicating and reinforcing the leadership narrative and the difference that the organisation is seeking to make, ensuring that all important connection with their employees and inclusivity in their message. In academy trusts, that must be more than woolly words such as 'providing the best education' or 'delivering an outstanding education', but instead a clear and inspiring view of what success looks like for children and young people of this generation, and the role of the trust and its work in making that a reality. This will inspire people both to join and to stay at the organisation – but the CEO must keep it up and find every opportunity to tell the story again and again. Building the leadership narrative into recruitment marketing literature is essential.

Aside from the importance of sense of purpose, which seems to almost universally be the key reason why people choose to join and stay with an employer, a recent survey by Deloitte found that areas such as 'the use made of skills'; 'variety of experiences', and 'professional development' all feature very closely behind in terms of what the new generation of workers are looking for. Again, a culture of 'talent spotting' and learning and development begins at the top.

The CEO is central to how the organisation engages its workforce, makes the most of their skills and connects them into the broader vision. This may be through performance management and leadership development systems, or through other, potentially more creative and innovative ways.

At the Keys Federation, an academy trust of four schools in Wigan, the CEO Sharon Bruton has created a scheme whereby people from all levels of the organisation are invited to apply for the role of 'Leaders of Purpose'. Candidates must put forward an initiative they have planned themselves, through which they can contribute their skills, talents and passions towards leading on a particular strategic priority. Staff have demonstrated high levels of motivation for developing their leadership skills and contributing to the wider success of the organisation, not least in areas such as improving the school environments, identifying opportunities for achieving better value for money, or engaging more girls in STEM subjects. Successful applicants are not paid any more money to do this work, they are simply motivated to contribute their ideas, time and further develop their leadership skills through initiatives that will benefit the wider organisation and pupils.

Elsewhere, REAch2 Academy Trust is developing its 11B411 initiative, which makes a commitment to providing every child within the trust access to 11 inspiring and enriching extra-curricula experiences before they leave primary school. The scheme is at the heart of putting the organisation's vision into practice. The key point is how it involves the trust's workforce in leading and delivering the scheme – drawing on the talents and ideas of staff at all levels, to create and provide its children with a wide range of new and exciting experiences of the world around them, raising their aspirations in the process. Where the talents and ideas of staff is recognised and made use of in such a way that connects with their sense of purpose, retention is almost always assured.

Of course, the CEO should also set the tone in terms of learning and professional development. They should ensure that the organisation has a clear and well-understood talent development framework and that they themselves are invested in it and supporting it, not least through their own learning. The same goes for their senior leaders and managers. A culture of coaching, mentoring and professional networking is particularly valued by the next generation of employees, but this kind of culture only takes hold if the most senior leaders encourage it and support it to flourish. Every CEO must value and be seen to value professional learning, development and growth. The best CEOs almost always have their own mentors, as we will see later in this book.

Values-based organisations

Finally, values are also crucial. Again, the CEO sets the tone both in living out the values and behaviours that make the organisation a positive and inspirational place to work. They also have a critical role in confronting those behaviours that fly in the face of the organisation's values. The recent example of alleged sexual abuse at Oxfam has shown how important it is for the senior leadership to not only be seen to be living the values, but to confront those whose behaviour is inconsistent with them. As the saying goes 'culture is defined by the worst behaviours leaders will tolerate'.

The CEO must be mindful of how they set the tone in this regard. People watch the CEO, intensely and unremittingly, for cues on what is acceptable and what is not. In the same way people watch to see who the CEO spends time with, and the parts of the business they spend the most time on to understand their priorities. People will also look carefully to see what behaviours the CEO confronts and addresses. People will undoubtedly ask themselves: 'what things can we get away with in this organisation, and what can we not get away with?'

Sadly, in a minority of organisations, including academy trusts, the CEO themselves have failed to live by the values. We began at the beginning of the book by considering the four foundations of the role and the fact that values, ethics and behaviours are key to a CEO's stable and successful tenure. Where they break the values, be it pursuing growth for growths' sake, engaging in commercial practices that are unethical and/or create conflicts of interest, or engaging in underhand tactics such as off-rolling or putting staff under overly intense pressure to improve results, the board should step in. Where the board doesn't step in, the organisation quickly becomes rotten, and, as we have seen with some academy trusts, will implode as a result.

However, for most CEOs this is about building on a firm foundational understanding of what their values and ethics (and also the organisation's values and ethics) are. Yet, we are all human. I have already written about the microscope under which CEOs increasingly live, and this is why living out the values matters even more in today's highly transparent world. A CEO must be even more mindful of their constituents and audiences.

As Rich McBee, CEO of Mitel since 2011, said in a recent business article: 'In today's world of instant communication and social media, it's easy to broadcast every single thought without an understanding of who it is reaching. It can also blur lines between your opinion and what your company stands for. If your stakeholders – customers, employees, investors, and so on – get wind of your views and don't agree, they may factor these views into decisions they make about you and your company. You need to carefully consider what you are saying and how it could be perceived by the various stakeholders, especially at a time when people are constantly trying very hard to read between the lines.'[36]

This is a difficult path to tread, and it does make the CEO role even more challenging and all consuming, with CEOs struggling to balance their private and personal lives. Yet, there is no getting away from the fact that the CEO is the figurehead of the organisation and this means that they are never off duty when it comes to living the values and ethics that their organisation embodies.

'Love' your staff

As well as providing their staff with a culture that empowers, develops, and supports their people, a CEO who 'loves' their staff goes a long way. This is no more evident than at moments where the stakes are high, and an organisation must change.

---

36. McBee, R. (14 October 2018) 'I've been a CEO for 7 years – here's the best advice I can give you about being successful in the role'. (Business Insider) Available at: www.businessinsider.com/how-to-be-a-great-ceo-2018-10?r=UK&IR=T

A CEO cannot know or build a professional relationship with everyone who works for his or her organisation. Yet they must recognise that their role and influence is such that each employee will feel some sort of emotional connection with the CEO, and most employees will have an opinion on how the CEO (or, at least, the leadership of the organisation), makes them feel. This is something to be very mindful about and a CEO should seek to connect as much as possible. It is not unusual – indeed, it is quite common – for many CEOs (with the help of executive support staff) to acknowledge the birthdays, key life events and individual successes of their staff.

Some of this is about leadership narrative, which we touched on in Chapter 3. The CEO must connect the organisation's direction with people's hopes, dreams and day-to-day experiences. However, this also has a very practical dimension, particularly in terms of whether employees are made to feel valued and cared for through organisational change and complexity. The temptation for all CEOs is to use their levers of power to make big and rapid changes in order to deliver results. As much as they can do, a CEO must provide a culture of safety and care for employees at all times, because when we feel high threat we simply do not perform. This is also about values.

As a recent article by INSEAD Knowledge stated: 'this core leadership practice becomes even more important at times of increasing complexity, which puts additional pressure on employees and may lead to stress and reduced performance.'[37]

A more thoughtful CEO will ask staff about their experiences and perceptions, involve them wherever possible in strategic planning, and look to make changes that take into account the needs of their staff and the people who they serve. They will bring people with them. Those CEOs who are setting the mitigation of workload as an organisational priority, for example, have done well to read the landscape and are now well placed to establish their trusts as employers of choice.

---

37. Shekshnia, S & Kravchenko, K. (9 May 2018) 'CEOs Should Be Chief Enablement Officers'. (INSEAD Knowledge.) Available at: https://knowledge.insead.edu/leadership-organisations/ceos-should-be-chief-enablement-officers-9056

As with values, a CEO that visibly prioritises their health and wellbeing, as well as the health and wellbeing of their staff, will set the tone. A great CEO can recruit and build a fabulous senior team, and, through them, a fabulous organisation of people; but if the health and wellbeing of the organisation's talent is not invested in, from the top down, it will not matter.

Recruitment and retention may currently be a challenge across the board in today's economy, including in the education system, but it will always be a priority for an effective CEO who will have developed the strategy, culture and relationships to ensure that people will always aspire to work for them and for their organisations.

Questions for reflection

- Are you building relationships across the sector with people who you would potentially – one day – like to hire to the most senior and influential positions in your organisations?

- Do you have an employer of choice strategy, with clear reference to research around the expectations of millennial and Generation Z employees?

- Are you investing sufficiently in retention: building a culture that identifies people's skills and interests, engages staff at all levels in activities that directly link to furthering the vision, and providing a clear framework for the talent management of all staff?

- Do you consult and involve staff early enough in major changes, seeking to understand the barriers and challenges they may face and seeking their input and suggestions for how change can be successful for all involved?

- Do you readily confront and challenge those behaviours that conflict with the organisation's values, whilst also celebrating those practices and achievements that strongly reflect them?

Chapter 6

Enabling improvement and innovation as an 'organisational habit'

'There's nothing you can't do if you get the habits right.'
- Charles Duhigg, *The Power of Habit: Why we do what we do and how to change*

The CEO should be an enabler, not a driver of improvement and innovation. This is probably the most significant shift for someone moving from successful director level leadership to Chief Executive Officer. Most will owe their position of CEO to the enormous success they have achieved in their field of expertise, having developed the skills, knowledge and expertise over many years. So, it comes as a surprise (even a shock) to many when becoming a CEO that their job in relation to improvement and innovation is now much more 'hands off and eyes on'.

In reality, the good CEO is a guiding hand and a lending hand to the team of experts and the organisation around them, rather than a busy or, dare I say it, 'meddling' hand. The reason for this is that most CEOs run large organisations – be it in terms of people, the scale of delivery, and/or geographical reach. It is physically and mentally impossible for them to drive improvement from 'the front'. If they do not make this change in mindset from the expert driving things forward to the enabler creating the right conditions for improvement and success, the job will feel 'undoable' and the organisation will lack sustainable leadership and the culture, capacity and behaviours for building a legacy.

The good CEO recognises that improvement at scale is not about the individual 'hero' leader or indeed a small group of expert people. It depends on improvement becoming what I describe as 'an organisational habit', driven by the culture, the processes and the people at all levels of the organisation.

So, the starting point, as we have seen so often in this book so far, is for the CEO to step back with humility at the size and scale of the task. They should look to consider the culture and behaviours within the organisation, its capacity, and the things that it prioritises and resources, in order to make a clear assessment as to whether the organisational habits actually reflect the CEO's narrative for what improvement should look like. The CEO must then look to changing the organisational habits if necessary, rather than drawing on the sheer force of their personality and personal graft to do so! Although a little bit of this, if dispensed with humility, can help.

How does this apply to academy trust CEOs?

At Forum Strategy we have worked hard to understand how multi academy trust CEOs can make the transition to working at scale. There are currently two kinds of MAT CEO, those who believe they themselves should be leading and delivering school improvement, and those who think they are responsible for enabling it. In trusts that are growing beyond two or three schools, and with every intention to work at an even greater scale, it is those CEOs who are focused on 'enabling improvement' that are best placed to succeed.

Many (not all) academy trust CEOs struggle to see why they should let go of the day to day leadership of improvement. Isn't their longstanding success in this area the reason why they were appointed as CEO? Well, yes and no. We have seen a number of highly capable leaders of school-to-school improvement struggle in the role of CEO. This is because they have either underestimated the sheer personal capacity that being actively involved in improvement across multiple schools requires, or they have focused too much on the improvement aspect of the job and neglected the other crucial parts of the role, including resourcing and external relationships. As I said in Chapter 1, the transition from lead professional to corporate leader is a bumpy one.

Does this mean that the CEO should disengage from improvement? Absolutely not. The effective CEO is entirely responsible for creating the priorities and the conditions for improvement. This is the improvement strategy; once they have shaped it, they should be ready to provide the necessary support and challenge to ensure it becomes a reality and continues to work effectively right across the trust.

There are numerous examples of where leaders have had to 'unleash' a culture of improvement and innovation in their organisation, often against their instincts if the organisation is struggling. One such example is the dramatic turnaround in the fortunes of the car manufacturer Fiat, and later the Fiat Chrysler group, under the leadership of the late Sergio Marchionne.

Despite having no previous experience of the car industry, Marchionne drew on his background as an accountant and tax specialist and was appointed as CEO of Fiat in 2004, tasked with turning around the company's seven billion dollar loss.

Marchionne set about trying to determine why the company was struggling. The outcome of this process clearly demonstrated to Marchionne that there was an ingrained management habit of upward referral, through many different layers. This not only critically delayed decision-making, but also was crippling innovation and preventing Fiat from keeping up with the developments of its rivals across the sector. Improvement and innovation was not an organisational habit; all activity needed to be sanctioned and directed through layers of management.

Whilst Marchionne was widely criticised for his subsequent dramatic actions in cutting huge swathes of the management and leadership layers across Fiat – and placing a greater onus on better communication and distributed ownership of improvement – the result was a much more efficient organisation. As a company, Fiat became much more adept at making rapid decisions and embracing creativity and innovation. As a result, they went on to develop the new Fiat 500, a modern reworking of the 1950s classic, which won European Car of the Year in 2008.

Marchionne found very similar problems when he became CEO of Chrysler in 2009 and set about re-energising an organisation where again the numerous bureaucratic layers had sapped employees' capacity for creativity and innovation. The creation of a much less hierarchical organisation, where people were trusted to make smart decisions and be accountable for their actions, led to a dramatic rebound in the organisation's success within four years. However, Marchionne had a clear message for staff at all times, that his actions and their work was not about the survival of the organisation, they were about purpose and sustainability. This is clearly set out in an email he sent to all Chrysler employees:

> 'The choice we have is between seeking only to build up our own organisation, or to develop a profitable enterprise that also promotes a better world. For my part, the choice is clear. The only way I can look at myself in the mirror every morning is if I know that sustainability is part of the very fabric of our business, and that we are helping create the conditions on which a positive future can emerge for our company, our children and humanity as a whole. Our success will be judged not only by what we do, but by how it is achieved.' – Sergio Marchionne, CEO Fiat Chrysler

What are the enabling factors for improvement and innovation at scale?

In response to the real challenge that some CEOs face in making the transition from driving improvement to enabling improvement at scale, we have developed a framework called the seven pillars of improvement. This provides CEOs with some principles to draw upon on here.

The seven pillars are:

1. The narrative for improvement

2. Capacity for improvement and innovation

3. Collective commitment

4. Robust and real time intelligence

5. Robust processes and project management

6. Investment in innovation and staying at 'the cutting edge'

7. Quality assurance of the improvement culture and model[38]

1. The narrative for improvement

First of all, the CEO must ensure that the improvement and innovation priorities align with and further the trust board's vision and strategy. In multi-academy trusts the most inspirational CEOs know that basing their improvement narrative on the government's accountability agenda alone is neither going to enthuse or inspire an organisation and its people to excel. They will look to embed these top/down measures within the improvement model, but they look beyond them and focus on other indicators and outputs. These will include improving the wellbeing of pupils and staff, the environment of their schools, the quality of the resources and the opportunities children have access to, academic outcomes across the board, the organisation's success as an employer of choice, the quality of the relationships the schools and the trust have with key stakeholders, and the sustainability of schools, both financially and operationally.

Indeed, most successful organisations will put customers' or end users' views at the heart of their improvement agenda, be it through sales feedback, quality of experience (reviews), or repeated engagement. Next will come the views and experiences of their staff, with organisations asking questions such as: how motivated and engaged they are, whether their attendance is good or not, and how engaged they are with professional development and innovation? Then will come the perceptions of the organisation in the general marketplace or the perceptions of regulators! (Many schools and trusts still put this first for obvious reasons.)

In creating a more 'rounded' narrative for improvement, a narrative they own rather than being imposed upon, the CEO already begins to shape an improvement culture by relating improvement to people's motivations. In

---

38. Forum Education Limited 2018

the case of most multi-academy trusts: enriching and improving children and young people's lives and educational experiences. It is worth noting that what a CEO believes should be measured often speaks volumes about their leadership, values and their openness to wider forms of accountability than simply 'the government'! Meanwhile, building staff motivation and wellbeing into the measure of organisational improvement is often a sign of an organisation that understands the basis of sustained success.

The danger is that we place the onus on measuring what is either fashionable or what, in the public sector at least, is imposed upon us as a measure of success. The same applies in the world of business and charities. Businesses and charities can become driven by factors that feel high stakes – such as meeting regulations or ensuring adequate funding and resources are in place. A business that is struggling can begin to measure improvement by how happy the bank managers are, and a charity can focus its improvement efforts solely on generating sufficient funding. In both cases, as with a multi-academy trust too focused on 'scores on the doors', this can become harmful if the people who will lead the improvement no longer feel connected to the organisational vision for improvement and improvement priorities.

Ultimately, a bank manager will only be pleased if a company is successful because its clients are happy and its end product is successful, meaning people will buy into the product or service. Indeed, it is this core work that motivates the people at the heart of improvement and innovation, not keeping a regulator or bank manager satisfied.

Top tips for CEOs on 'narrative for improvement':

- Regularly revisit the narrative for improvement with all key stakeholders, with strong reference to how this manifests itself through the experiences of customers/end users. Ask, what does success look like and how can the organisation achieve it through innovation and improvement? Talk about 'our vision' rather than 'my vision'.

- Review your improvement model to ensure KPIs reflect the narrative for the success and the 'best' end user experience, not simply the accountabilities placed upon us by regulators or bank managers. Remember – 'what gets measured tends to get done'.

- Communicate and reinforce the narrative constantly, and carefully connect it to people's roles, responsibilities and accountabilities at all levels of the organisation. Does the narrative come through clearly enough through your organisational communications?

2. Capacity for improvement and innovation

Once the priorities are set (and they may change depending on the context), the effective CEO ensures that the organisation is building the capacity to deliver as an organisational habit – without their day to day involvement in operations. Stuart Conroy, CEO of Activ8 Distribution and a Sunday Times Fast-Track Award winner, talks about this shift in mindset:

'In the early days of growth it is about recognising the shift – that you now need people around you who are more expert and skilled in certain areas of delivery than you are to lead operations. It's not just about getting in different professional experience, such as HR or legal advice, it's about having people on board who can lead the delivery and sales of the core product to the highest standards on your behalf.'

In essence, this requires a significant degree of letting go and means equipping and trusting others to take on the day-to-day leadership of improvement and innovation. To further test his commitment to this, in the summer of 2018, Stuart did something that many CEOs would balk at. After a period of preparation, he physically stepped away from the organisation for a few months to see how well the culture, systems and processes worked without him. To his relief, it worked! But that decision to step away was based on his long-held commitment to developing the capacity and commitment amongst his senior team, as well as embedding the necessary systems and processes, to deliver to the highest standards.

Good CEOs know that the leadership of improvement is not the same as the delivery of improvement, so they work hard to create capacity in both areas. For the CEO, it is crucial they have 'improvement leadership' capacity on their senior teams; people who are hugely experienced in leading the delivery of improvement and innovation and are 'the best of the best' in terms of the frontline aspect of the work. In the academy trust world there are still very few people in the system for CEOs to draw upon who have genuine experience of leading school improvement across multiple sites (as opposed to delivering school to school support on the ground).

In securing leadership for improvement and innovation, effective CEOs are very careful in taking their time to recruit people with the necessary skills for 'leading' as opposed to simply 'delivering' improvement. Being an improvement specialist is not the same as being an improvement leader in a large organisation, but the improvement leader must have grounding as a specialist. Indeed, it's crucial for the CEO to be very clear on the difference between what we describe as a 'leader of school improvement' and a 'deliverer' of it. So, how do the two roles differ?

Executive-level leadership and school improvement leadership:

- Experience of delivering whole-scale school improvement successfully
- Analytical skills
- Project management skills
- Brokerage skills
- Influencing and lateral thinking skills
- Quality assurance/ability to hold others to account
- Coaching/mentoring skills
- Stakeholder management skills

School improvement delivery:

- Specific professional expertise
- Coaching/mentoring skills
- Relationship building skills
- Research skills

The effective CEO will ensure that leaders in these respective roles have the necessary skills and experience, and, where they are lacking, that they are receiving the necessary experience, training and support. It is so important that their improvement leaders can make the step up – and this is often a chicken or egg situation as so many are still very new to the role. In particular, the effective CEO will fully depend on their improvement leaders to design and deliver robust project management processes which embed goal setting, project planning, the brokerage of improvement and innovation delivery, and on-going quality assurance across the organisation.

In terms of academy trusts, these elements are all essential for a school improvement model that operates at scale, but strong project management skills are not easy to come by even amongst some of our most experienced school leaders.

To bolster capacity further, many organisations look at undertaking systematic talent audits of their staff in order to identify skills and experience that may not be obvious based on their current role or responsibilities. This is crucial for a CEO and senior team who, because of scale, simply cannot be expected to talent spot potential leaders and experts personally. A CEO should ask, does the organisation have the systems and process in place in order to know its staff well enough and, through that, provide them with the necessary development to generate more capacity for improvement and innovation? Remember, this is not about you as the leader knowing everyone's strengths – it is about you ensuring that the organisation's systems capture this.

Top tips for CEOs looking to build capacity for improvement and innovation:

- Before scaling up, ensure that sufficient school improvement and innovation leadership roles are in place, removing the day-to-day responsibility for this from the CEO. Recruit carefully, looking for experience but also – crucially – for the key skills and competencies necessary to lead improvement and innovation at scale.

- Invest in the on-going professional development of less experienced employees, including preparation for leadership of – as well as delivery of – improvement projects creating an internal improvement leadership pipeline.

- Maintain sensible geographical distances between sites where possible that allow for expertise and resources for improvement to be easily shared.

3. Collective commitment

If improvement is going to be an organisational habit, everyone in the organisation must have a strong sense of team. In talking about the Formula 1 pit stops, David Coulthard describes the camaraderie as thus: 'The team is very tight-knit, there is a strong sense of interdependence; we work together to win together, lose together, and be safe together.'

For CEOs and leaders running multiple sites, divisions and departments, building that sense of 'togetherness' and commitment to collective success can be enormously challenging. When an organisation grows to scale, things become less 'tight-knit', and generating a collective commitment can become a much-prized skill amongst CEOs. Indeed, some organisations embrace this lack of collective commitment and create a sense of competition between their respective sites, departments and divisions to 'spur' improvement. That is not something I would recommend at all. But it is a culture that can readily creep if we are not careful.

There are some 'soft' and 'hard' approaches that CEOs can take to fostering a culture of collective commitment.

From a 'soft' perspective, they can readily look to their leadership narrative in order to create a sense of 'togetherness' and being an organisational whole. The narrative should demonstrate the impact and influence of the whole organisation and the difference it makes to society and to the people it serves. Connecting employees and specific aspects of the organisation's work into that narrative, and enabling employees to see how the contribution they make is interdependent with that of others, is a very powerful way of doing this.

I know of one CEO, Helen Rowland of Focus Trust (see Appendix 2) who has worked hard to embed a culture of collective commitment as her organisation grew to fifteen schools. Her leadership narrative began to embed a very important mantra: 'we are only as successful as our weakest school.' Creating that sense of togetherness and responsibility to one another is key, and Helen began from a position of shared values and a shared sense of 'the business we are in', to connect people into the wider organisational vision for collective improvement. There was an onus on empowering and encouraging leaders and teams across all schools to contribute towards improvement and innovation across the wider trust – moving responsibility and ownership from the centre to all facets of the organisation. As outlined at the beginning of this chapter, Helen's approach is not that dissimilar to the one that Sergio Marchionne took.

There are also 'hard' ways of creating a sense of collective commitment to organisational improvement and innovation too. Employees – starting with the senior leadership team – can have measures included within their performance management metrics that relate to cross-organisational outcomes, the success against which depends on cross-organisational team effort and commitment. Recruitment processes and person specifications can also be geared towards recruiting those candidates who demonstrate an understanding of the organisation's wider vision and work, and encourage candidates to demonstrate how they would commit to organisation wide success.

How does this relate to multi-academy trusts?

A key premise of successful multi-academy trusts is their ability to draw upon and mobilise the skills and talents of staff across their schools to achieve improvements in more schools and for more children. Indeed, sustainable and successful school improvement models depend not only on sufficient professional expertise and sound and scalable improvement processes, but also, crucially, on the capacity of a wide-range of professionals to provide coaching, mentoring, CPD, peer review, and – at times – substantive leadership or teaching support.

Yet, challenges and barriers to collective school improvement can easily present themselves. Achieving cultural commitment to whole-trust success, in a context where leaders are highly accountable for individual schools, can be challenging. Leaders are also – quite rightly – invested emotionally and professionally in 'their schools'. Finding a balance, however, is key to the collective success of all schools and all children in academy trusts.

Where this is overcome, and a sense of collective commitment is achieved, the potential for academy trusts to galvanise the expertise, skills and capacity for school improvement at scale is significant. As Helen Rowland, CEO of Focus Trust, says: 'we began to see leaders deepen their commitment and their enthusiasm for supporting other academies. Principals were more ready and willing to release their deputies and assistant heads for secondments in other schools – which is a big ask at times – because it was increasingly recognised as being part of our trust's moral imperative.' Indeed, such generosity has played a crucial role in the recent improvement of a number of schools in challenging circumstances and has also seen senior and middle leaders develop their leadership skills. Principals are also using the secondment of their staff as an opportunity to promote high potential middle leaders for periods of time to gain experience and development, which further builds the organisation's capacity for improvement.

Top tip for CEOs in generating collective commitment:

- Generating commitment fundamentally depends on engaging leaders and teachers with a compelling leadership for achieving the best organisational – rather than departmental or divisional – improvement and innovation outcomes. However, there are also some key levers that can ensure commitment to the wider organisation's success – including performances targets, recruitment, maintaining geographical proximity between sites, and an emphasis on networking and cross-site working amongst staff.

4. Robust and real time intelligence

A CEO also depends enormously on robust and 'real time' data intelligence to create a culture where improvement and innovation is an organisational habit. It is crucial that a CEO shapes the systems and processes of data capture and intelligence gathering that give them the confidence to monitor, analyse, review and challenge trends and risks, challenges and opportunities across the organisation. Just as importantly, we must remember that 'what gets measured gets done', and the CEO must recognise that the activities and outputs they – indirectly or otherwise – deem as important through being captured through the organisation's reporting and evaluation systems, will be prioritised by leaders, managers and staff at all levels of the organisation. The CEO must choose very carefully what gets measured.

It is important that these systems of reporting include a number of elements: they are regular and routine; the routines are well understood and adhered to by all involved in data capture and reporting; all those involved in gathering intelligence and data are sufficiently trained to undertake the task; intelligence is captured from a range of sources – providing a sufficient degree of triangulation; and the processes of data capture and reporting are workable and purposeful.

Adherence to the routine of reporting is essential to keeping a large improvement organisation ticking (and the CEO and senior leadership team, as well as the board where appropriate, informed). Indeed, the reporting of priority data should be a standard operating procedure, a non-negotiable for all leaders and others involved in its capture. However, this should be tempered with a commitment to making intelligence gathering and data capture manageable – ensuring that the quest for intelligence does not in itself impact on leaders' and practitioners' ability to actually do the job and, therefore, present a risk to standards. Again, reliance on a few individuals to capture data is not characteristic of a scalable improvement model.

This is partly overcome by the importance of using a range of sources to gather intelligence and data. Depending on the same sources or conduits of information is a characteristic of smaller trusts and organisations to rely on one or two individual leaders for both improvement and quality assurance expertise, and it is important that this reliance is addressed as MATs move to scale.

The journalist and war veteran Donald McLachlan once wrote that 'reliance on one source is dangerous, the more reliable and comprehensive the source, the greater the danger'. McLachlan was writing here about the lessons learned from World War II, where Germany became almost exclusively reliant on spy networks in England and the Middle East that were actually controlled by the Allies. As the military writer Michael Handel says: 'the corroboration of any potentially valuable information by other independent verifiable sources such as air reconnaissance, radio and radars, and different sensors is imperative. In retrospect, Germany's decision to rely so heavily on one (or few) sources is astounding.'[39]

39. Handel, M. (2004) *Strategic and Operational Deception in the Second World War (Studies in Intelligence)* Abingdon, Oxon: Frank Cass.

How does this apply to multi-academy trusts?

A CEO of a multi-academy trust depends enormously on the data they receive in order to monitor the organisation's on-going improvement – including the risks, challenges, failures and successes. CEOs that do not have a handle on the data or are not receiving a wide enough range of data in a timely enough fashion soon lose touch with the organisation.

It is important that a MAT CEO has access to:

- **Regular summaries of data:** ensuring that data is 'real time' and can be used to anticipate and address challenges, not simply in order to respond to them once they have set in. This means that data isn't simply about reporting, but that it is part of the lifeblood of improvement activity. A culture where data is simply about accountability – summative, rather than formative if you will – leads to a position where people are less willing to speak openly about risk, challenge and what can be done to improve. Positive data also needs to be captured quickly in order to identify and mobilise innovative practices that can benefit the organisation more widely.

- **Triangulated data:** MATs must ensure that their monitoring and reporting models build in the inputs of a range of sources and conduits of intelligence. This could include regular anonymous surveys of staff to gather views on workforce motivation, wellbeing, professional development and their perceptions of school performance; admissions data (always a good sign of whether improvement is taking effect or not and easily accessible); peer review undertaken by other schools either within or even beyond the MAT (beyond can bring more independence); parental surveys; and putting sufficient onus on the reporting role of the Local Advisory/Governing Board. This is also why it is so important that the CEO works with the board to ensure that the scheme of delegation does not create substantial overlap between school improvement leaders and the local governing boards of schools. The CEO must be able to refer to governing boards for insight and challenge, without sensing conflict.

- **Put the end-user at the heart of intelligence gathering:** To ensure we maintain and enhance the focus on children and young people through growth, it is also key that MATs not only listen to them, but take on board their views as 'customers' and as agents of improvement itself. As Adam Sewell-Jones of NHS Improvement told our MAT Leaders network in the East Midlands recently 'keeping the customers' voice – be they patients or children – at the heart of the improvement process is key'. This is, arguably, something that many other sectors are far better at than education, and it must be a priority as the MAT grows and, inevitably, its senior leaders become that little more distant from the 'day-to-day' experience at the chalk face. Indeed, children and young people are a great, but often untapped, source of intelligence for school improvement.

Top tips for the CEO in ensuring robust and 'real time' data and intelligence:

- Ensure that the customers' voice – that of children and young people in academy trusts – is heard as part of the intelligence gathering process. Children and customers provide a unique and very honest perspective, and they can be drawn upon to provide very honest feedback that is like gold dust in informing improvement and innovation.

- Ensure that the organisational improvement model builds in clear and non-negotiable routines and expectations for data capture, from a wide-range of sources.

- Ensure there is sufficient standardisation of reporting so that clear comparisons can be made between sites and groups/ regions in order to inform improvement and innovation activity.

5. Robust processes and project management

Leaders of small organisations (and trusts) are able to lean on personal and proximate relationships to set expectations and guarantee on-going behaviours and communications that drive improvement. These leaders can – to an extent – drive the process: personally challenging the data, undertaking the coordination and planning of improvement, modelling the behaviours, and providing the quality assurance as they go. In larger organisations, that simply isn't possible. It certainly isn't for the CEO.

Why does process matter so much? Improvement and innovation at scale requires a model where people at all levels and across a wide number of sites have a clear and shared understanding about the improvement model they are operating within, are confident in their own role in contributing to the improvement process when required and know how to act accordingly. Process matters enormously for ensuring that a large organisation can react and respond to the data and intelligence it is gathering. This is the essence of improvement and innovation as an organisational habit.

Why is that? It is because process creates the all important organisational behaviours and traits, including the most important one of all: learning. In his book *Black Box Thinking*, Matthew Syed talks about the aviation industry as a 'growth mindset' industry: 'they hire talented people but they have realised that talent is not enough. They have to learn, they have to engage with the data, with the opportunities that can drive them towards a better safety record.' In aviation, when a near miss takes place, clear standard operating procedures fall into place. 'Both pilots voluntary submit a report and the totality of these reports is statistically analysed to understand the weakness that lead to these accidents and to make the relevant reforms.' Concerning (and indeed positive) data and intelligence is not simply taken at face value but is instead subjected to the significant scrutiny and interrogation of a wide range of experts, who then prescribe a suitable way forward. This is the important transition from pillar 4 into pillar 5.

For scalable improvement this means ensuring that follow up diagnosis becomes a standard operating procedure (SOP) where our robust and real-time intelligence demands it. It is at this point – through carefully developed SOPs – that you expand the process beyond individual leaders. Such a SOP should ensure the right people are immediately deployed to review the issue in greater depth rather than making assumptions that may lead to the wrong course of action. Those reviewing the data should immediately be able to show that the risk has not only been identified but that its causes are – as a result – being carefully understood and that an evidence-based course of action is being prescribed. We would also add that a system should be in place for enabling the findings to be disseminated to other leaders and practitioners across the organisation, ensuring that others can learn the lessons and prevent further issues elsewhere.

It is this organisational (or in this case, sector-wide mindset) that has driven improvement in aviation safety to the point of record levels in 2017. According to Syed, it all comes down to 'decades of institutionalised learning – driven by a responsibility to learn in a complex world, a recognition that talent isn't enough, has driven an incredible safety record. At the beginning of the last century aviation was the riskiest form of transportation – but in 2014, for the major airlines, there was one crash for every 8.3 million take-offs.'[40]

The message here is that relying on talent is not enough. A CEO needs to foster a culture (underpinned by a process) that makes it a non-negotiable to confront the brutal facts – the concerning intelligence as it arises – quickly. Processes can ensure that we are identifying risks and engaging numerous professionals in providing their perspectives in securing a diagnosis of the issues that lie behind the data (good or bad). Indeed, successful organisations will not only seek to provide an accurate diagnosis of risks and challenges, but also of success. As Sir Michael Barber says:

'If the data comes in fast enough for the system to be able to respond in time, and if those using the data have the right 'can do' mindset, then problems can be solved before they become crises or outright failures.'[41]

Peer review within MATs can be an excellent way of providing that initial diagnosis of the issues behind concerning intelligence. Many MATs are now building the peer review process within the front-end of their school improvement processes, ensuring that the focus of review is driven by what the intelligence is telling them is an area of concern.

40. London Business Forum (2017) *Matthew Syed – Black Box Thinking*. [Video] Available at: www.youtube.com/watch?v=-r0avhWk-xk
41. Barber, M. (2008) *Instruction to Deliver: Fighting to Transform Britain's Public Services*. London, England: Methuen Publishing.

In any case, MATs should be able to deploy people with the skills and experience to provide the necessary depth and rigor of diagnosis. The process of diagnosis itself should be clear and evidence based.

Questions for reflection

- Does your MAT put sufficient onus on diagnosing the issues and practices that lie behind concerning or positive data? Are there standard operating procedures in place to reinforce a commitment to undertaking sufficiently detailed diagnosis?

- Are you dependent on one or a small group of leaders to engage in diagnosis, or are you able to consult multiple professional opinions and encourage sufficient challenge – potentially through peer review?

- Are your heads, SLEs and other expert practitioners sufficiently trained in diagnosis and review in order to provide the capacity and skills for diagnosis at scale?

- Do you have standard operating procedures for sharing the outcomes of a diagnosis to ensure other schools, leaders and practitioners can learn from mistakes made or excellent practice in other schools?

Goal-setting and planning

The process for all improvement activity must then ensure that diagnosis translates into a plan of action. In his book, *Instruction to Deliver*, the former head of the Prime Minister's delivery unit, Sir Michael Barber, discusses some of the crucial elements to delivering improvement, including the following four:

- Setting goals
- Plans
- The delivery chain
- Stocktakes

Goal setting is crucial. It ensures that there is a clear focus and success criteria for improvement activity and it remains sufficiently ambitious. This is where the influence of vision (pillar 1) is so important.

Goal setting must be carefully informed by a number of factors, not least the diagnosis, but also by benchmarking with other schools within the trust and through dialogue with all those who are likely to be involved in improvement activity. Indeed, it must involve all parties, those providing leadership, those providing school improvement delivery, those providing quality assurance, and the school's headteacher and local governing body.

Too many goals can be dangerous. Trying to change too much at the same time can lead to a lack of focus, to leaders and practitioners being overwhelmed, and to an ability to pinpoint what may be driving improvement or continued failures. So goals, as well as being SMART (Specific, Measurable, Attainable, Relevant, and Time-limited) and ambitious, should also be tight and focused.

Goals should also be publicly stated where its possible, at least amongst staff within the trust, to encourage a sense of shared understanding, commitment, accountability, and transparency around the improvement process.

The plan itself is the key driver of delivery activity. Again, it should be clear, with specific details in terms of a timeframe of actions and reference to who is responsible for which aspect of delivery (with reference to costings and interdependencies). It should also have detailed SMART objectives that clearly link to the overarching goals so that the school improvement work can be readily reviewed for impact through the stocktakes and quality assured.

In Instruction to Deliver, Sir Michael Barber explains how the expectation that government departments would have plans to drive particular aspects of improvement was, at the time (early 2000s), so revolutionary, yet also so fundamental to improvement initiatives carrying momentum: 'There was nothing original about what we wanted. We were simply asking for standard practice in the management of programmes and projects, a discipline that emerged from engineering in the 20th century and became second nature across most of business. Applying programme and project management does not guarantee success, but it does ensure, if applied rigorously, that crucial details will not be missed, and emerging problems will be identified earlier.'

Barber judged the improvement planning of each government department by asking the following questions?

- Did they have a credible plan?
- Did they have arrangements for overseeing the implementation of their plan?
- Would they know soon enough if insufficient progress was being made or if something was going horribly wrong?

How does this apply to multi-academy trusts?

So how are academy trusts building standard programme and project management practice into the processes which underpin their school improvement models? One of the most impressive I have come across is that of The Flying High Trust and it is encouraging to see some other trusts adopting similar models. A full case study of Flying High's improvement model is included in Appendix 3.

Flying High ensure that their school improvement delivery is driven by a document called The Individual School Action Plan (ISAP), which sets out the level and nature of school improvement that each school requires (informed by a wide range of data and intelligence), and provides a clear overview of who is involved and responsible for achieving improvement and by when. The action plans evolve in response to the information gathered through regular quality assurance visits and other data/intelligence, and are the key documents ensuring that everyone involved is clear about a school's improvement priorities and plans. The school's headteacher, Director of QA, and the Director of the Teaching School Alliance are all involved in writing and agreeing the ISAP (together with setting key targets and agreeing costings of school improvement).

The delivery chain and stocktakes

It must be noted here that the delivery chain is an important aspect in setting out the plan as it encourages leaders of school improvement to consider all those potential influencers on the improvement process and how they can seek to ensure that each has the necessary capacity, expertise, support and/or information to help secure improvement.

From the improvement delivery perspective, this clearly involves engaging appropriate school improvement specialists from across the trust's schools (and potentially beyond) and ensuring that they understand the goals and the plan and are well supported to deliver and to collaborate with other colleagues and stakeholders involved. An important thing to consider here is talent auditing – understanding where expertise sits within the trust and ensuring that data is up to date. This data should sit in a database so that trust leaders can rapidly identify those individuals who can bring about improvement. Pillars 6 and 7 considers the importance of training, research and quality assurance of experts providing school improvement, which is also a key consideration here.

However, beyond the identification and deployment of experts, the plan should consider all those levers – hard and soft – that can be maximised to increase, as far as possible, the chances of the improvement initiative being a success. This can involve considering any need for training of staff, investment or engagement in research, additional resources, informing the focus of performance management objectives, and, indeed, seconding staff or engaging external consultancy where appropriate. Of course, missing one element may be enough to overlook a key driver of improvement.

Throughout the improvement process, real time, robust and triangulated intelligence must be continually sought (see detail with reference to pillar 4 – intelligence). Barber describes the use of real time data as being crucial to maintaining sufficient momentum and challenge – highlighting the work of celebrated Police Chief Bill Bratton who dramatically reduced crime in New York through challenging and informing the learning of his precinct commanders through weekly data from precincts across the city. Indeed, the on-going reference to robust, real time data is key to the use of stocktakes throughout the process.

Stocktakes are a key element of the improvement process and should be a routine and non-negotiable operating procedure. This is because they ensure that momentum and accountability is maintained throughout the improvement process, and that key barriers and risks can be identified in a timely manner. Again, this is something many trusts are now developing as part of individual school improvement plans, ensuring trust boards and senior leaders are regularly and routinely monitoring specific improvement priorities throughout the year, rather than waiting until the end of the process to judge its success. I have written earlier about how people watch closely how a CEO uses their time. When Tony Blair was concerned about a particular government department or initiative, he would join Barber at a stocktake with the relevant department. The impact of this could not be overestimated and it is important that a CEO sometimes simply uses their time and presence to send a message that an improvement activity is particularly 'high stakes' and to ensure that people are aware of how vitally important their efforts and energies on a particular issue are to the organisation's overall success. It is also important to a CEO's leadership and the refinement of their leadership narrative to spend time within the improvement delivery model itself, to see the impact of the process and actions being taken, and to understand how people engage with it and genuinely feel about it.

There is one final point to add around process. The **improvement model** should be clearly articulated to all. A school improvement model that is too complicated or inaccessible is going to lead to disengagement. People need to know where they fit in to the process. They also need to know how others fit in to facilitate the sharing of information and to encourage a culture of support and collective commitment. This can be achieved in the obvious ways, through clear illustrations of the model and through informative induction for all school leaders and key staff. However, more engagingly, the use of case studies and showcasing of improvement practice can also help to raise awareness and bring to life the MATs improvement so that staff can both relate to it and also embrace it, rather than be fearful of it.

6. Investment in innovation and staying at the 'cutting edge'

The CEO will also ensure that sufficient resource is invested in research and development activity, including on-going staff training. Again, this should be aligned with the improvement priorities set out by the CEO as part of the improvement strategy.

The Global Innovation 1000 shows that the top organisations in the world are investing more and more in research and development activity (upwards of 5% of overall revenue), reflecting the importance of knowledge and evidence in driving innovation and improvement. I believe that we will increasingly see a gulf between those MATs who are investing significantly in developing their improvement activity based on evidence and those who aren't. An effective MAT CEO should be brave enough to pursue this investment despite the challenging financial climate – not least by working with other MATs with similar improvement needs and priorities. These organisations will be also able to respond far quicker and far more efficiently to the changing contexts they face.

Investment can be about both money and time. It is worth describing the way in which some organisations approach this.

An important aspect to this is providing people with the space and environment in which innovation can thrive. This requires the endorsement of the CEO, who must prize innovation and be willing to allow people to invest time and resource in it, whilst ensuring it remains disciplined and focused on the needs of end users.

In pursuing innovation it is important to break down silos – so that people can share and refine ideas and co-create. Many academy trusts are establishing networks of leaders and teachers across schools to develop new curriculum resources, to undertake planning and to research approaches to pedagogy in order to achieve improvement. In some cases this is being done to a very advanced level, with some trusts and schools undertaking randomised control trials on approaches to providing feedback to pupils and the best use of assistant teachers in lessons. Some of these trials, such as those undertaken by the Kyra Research School in Lincolnshire, have demonstrated improvements over time. Those improvements would not have been possible without the time, investment, and resources required to provide the space and framework for research-informed innovation to take place.

Innovation must be focused and disciplined – defined by the leadership narrative and the vision for improvement and innovation that aligns with the wider organisational vision. As we have seen, organisations like the Keys Federation and REAch2 have empowered their people to devise and lead on certain projects that align with the organisation's wider strategy and direction, and draw on research. These individuals have been given the space to be creative, to test ideas and to do things differently because they know that the projects are born out of a particular need that if addressed will contribute to 'the business we are in'.

Undisciplined innovation and a disconnection with 'the business we are in' led to the challenges faced by Lego discussed in Chapter 1. Between 1993 and 2004 Lego experienced hard times, with a general deterioration in sales and revenues; the company produced more products, but sales did not increase. In response to this disastrous decline the company laid off 1000 employees.

The company has continued to 'innovate', creating many new products, but it had failed to stay focused on the business it was in. The innovation was undisciplined.

The company's CEO went back to the heart of its work. Rather than hunker down and steady the ship, the new CEO, Knudstorp, embraced innovation – this time aligned to the company's core business. He had Lego invested in a kind of research the company had never done before – detailed ethnographic studies of how children around the world really play – and set up The Future Lab, a secretive and highly ambitious research and development team tasked with inventing new, technologically enhanced 'play experiences' for children all over the world. As Knudstorp puts it, '[Future Lab] is about discovering what's obviously Lego, but has never been seen before.'

He also created Lego Ideas, which is a crowdsourcing platform that allows fans to design their own sets, gather support from fellow fans (you need at least 10,000 votes) and eventually get Lego to produce your set as one of its standard lines.

Essentially Lego invested in the time, space and research to understand its audience and their expectations in a changing world.

This emphasis on the importance of research-informed creativity paid off. In 2006, Lego was named the world's sixth largest toy maker, with revenue at £717 million, an 11% increase from the previous year. Net profit for 2006 was £123.5 million, a jump of 6.5% over 2005.

In undertaking the Global Innovation 1000 in 2018,[42] PWC highlighted six key characteristics of both 'high-leverage innovators' and the larger universe of companies that report comparatively high performance vs. their peers. These characteristics (set out below) not only reflect the importance of disciplined innovation – with projects being closely aligned to the organisation's strategic priorities and the needs of its end-users – but also the need for innovation to be supported and promoted by senior leaders.

These all, in my view, begin with the CEO and their role in encouraging and guiding a culture of innovation.

1. Close alignment of innovation and business strategy

2. Company-wide cultural support for innovation

3. Close involvement with innovation program by leadership

4. Deep understanding of insights from end-users

5. Rigorous approach to research and development project selection

6. Ability to integrate all of these things together to create a unique experience

7. Quality assurance of the improvement culture and model

Finally, ultimately, it is the trust board who must hold the improvement model to account against the vision and their definition of success. It is therefore important that the accountable CEO is themselves constantly involved in learning about improvement and models of improvement, refining their strategy and approach in response to challenges and failures. The CEO must model a commitment to learning and must be the first to acknowledge failure and – just as importantly – the need to learn from it. The trust board should expect this and, throughout growth of the MAT, should expect the model to evolve further as the executive team test the model and prepare it for even greater scale.

42. Strategy& (2018) '2018 Global Innovation 1000: What the Top Innovators Get Right'. Available at: www.strategyand.pwc.com/media/file/2018-Global-Innovation-1000-Fact-Pack.pdf

This is, of course, about monitoring the outcomes of improvement initiatives and that the improvement model is achieving the goals set within the organisation's improvement narrative. However, in a sector that is still so young, it is also important to seek external quality assurance and challenge from credible peers. One way in which this is being achieved already is through MAT to MAT peer review. At Forum Strategy we have been impressed by MATs that have engaged in our peer review model in order to learn more about one another's improvement models and to provide constructive professional challenge on what may be improved – not least by interviewing those who work at the heart of the improvement model itself. One trust we worked with clearly had more to do to ensure that its model (as a whole) was well understood by those across the organisation that engaged with different parts of it. There was a risk that silos may emerge and that those delivering improvement did not understand how their role contributed to that of others or to wider improvement goals. As a result, the trust has worked hard on articulating its improvement model – bringing together the various elements within one document which informs the induction and on-going training of all those involved in cross-trust improvement.

MAT CEOs must get out there to see how other trusts are doing improvement, and how other sectors do it too. There is a wealth of information and learning from organisations such as the Care Quality Commission, NHS Improvement and various other sources who have been addressing the issue of improvement at scale for many years now. Our recent MAT Leaders networks have involved input from NHS Improvement whose CEO, Jim Mackey, spoke about the importance of improvement that is based on both 'mission and method'. For MAT CEOs, bridging the two and ensuring they are achieved in harmony is their key school improvement responsibility. They are not the first to face this task, and should be looking to other MATs and organisations beyond the sector for inspiration and insight.

Chapter 7

Sustainability and compliance

'Two roads diverged in a wood, and I - took the one less travelled by, and that has made all the difference.'

– Robert Frost

If you are a CEO leading an organisation in the public or charities sector, the issue of organisational sustainability will undoubtedly be very high on your agenda. Indeed, it probably pervades everything you do. The current funding restraints, with their roots going back to the financial crisis of 2008, mean that CEOs must be highly engaged in ensuring the medium and long-term viability of their organisations. Such is the challenge that the very survival of organisations is at stake, not simply the quality of the services they provide.

It is no exaggeration to say that the financial crash and the subsequent austerity in public funding (and restraint in private sector spending) has redefined and will continue to define the leadership priorities of this generation of CEOs. As I said – rather soberly – in my speech to Forum Strategy's national CEO conference in September 2018, just days after the British Prime Minister Theresa May had declared an end to austerity:

'The financial crash of 2008 changed everything. A growing aging population changes everything. Growing demands on public services changes everything. Brexit changes everything. The tighter public funding budgets will not go away. We need to find better ways of generating and maximising resources, not simply to cut across the board or live in hope for more cash later.'

However, with or without tighter funding, an entrepreneurial CEO will always look to maximise the resources available to them to achieve the greatest impact. As with the recruitment and retention challenges currently faced by all sectors, a good crisis always focuses minds, but really good CEOs remain 'alive' to these important strategic issues whether the context is one of high stakes or relative stability. That way, they are better prepared when challenges do take place – refusing to be complacent or comfortable in 'times of plenty' and then need to make knee jerk and often costly changes in strategy further down the road. They build roofs whilst the sun is shining.

So how do good CEOs approach this fundamental issue of sustainability and viability in times of hardship? Rather than guard every penny for use only when essential services need to be met, what we are instead seeing is an approach that guarantees long-term viability requires leaders to invest – strategically, and, undoubtedly, with some risk – in the development and evolution of their organisations. That often feels counter-intuitive – but only that way will CEOs continue to achieve the innovation necessary for realising better economies of scale and continue to meet their users' needs in an ever changing and complex world.

As someone who has grown a 'start-up' organisation with little resource to begin with to one operating nationally and supporting over one hundred organisations, I had to tread this tightrope carefully in the early days. The best piece of advice I received in growing my organisation was this: 'Don't waste money on things that do not add value either directly or indirectly or end up as liabilities in the long run when there are other options. Cut those things. But, invest also! Invest – as far as you can – with a long-term view, in the people, the resources, the systems and the partnerships that will provide a dividend to your clients and, therefore, to you for years to come.'

This advice has held me in good stead, but it meant spending some money with a view to the medium- to long-term, 'growing acorns' as it were, which isn't easy when budgets are tight. Making the right investments and taking calculated risks in doing things differently and more efficiently is a challenging, but essential, task for anyone leading in this climate.

This is a delicate balancing act, and it is one that is proving extremely challenging for CEOs across the board. Recent research by Charities Aid Foundation and the Association of Chief Executives of Voluntary Organisations found that charity leaders' biggest challenges in 2018 centred around generating more income and achieving financial sustainability whilst meeting demand for services and a reduction in public and government funding.[43] To generate that income and sustainability, we cannot simply rely on the old models to give birth to the new ones – some risk, innovation, and investment is required.

Managing this is probably the defining challenge for the current generation of public and charity sector CEOs.

Sustainability begins with the mindset of board and the ability of your team

For the CEO of a small and growing organisation this means two things. First of all, they need the backing of their board in taking a strategic rather than a protectionist or 'steady as she goes' approach to managing austerity and a tight financial climate. As David Strudley, a long time children's hospice CEO who experienced and successfully responded to the grave impact that the crash had on that sector in 2008, says: 'sustainable organisational development begins with the board – the changes required are often radical and highly strategic in nature, and that means the CEO often needs the necessary backing and support that such change requires.'[44]

If the board isn't willing to empower and support the CEO to invest strategically and with creativity in the short-term in order to reap

---

43. CAF. (2017) 'Social Landscape 2017'. Available at: www.cafonline.org/about-us/publications/2017-publications/social-landscape-2017
44. Forum Strategy. (13 December 2018) 'Policy Roundtable Report 3: Sustainability through an age of austerity'. Available at: www.forumstrategy.org/policy-roundtable-3-sustainability-through-an-age-of-austerity/

economies of scale and more efficient services in the long-term, the organisation will flounder. This will often be the case where a board is very much focused on balanced budgets and the bottom line year on year. For government-funded organisations this is a trap that is difficult to avoid.

What we see here is the need for boards to not simply focus on ploughing on to deliver the 'business we are in' – increasingly narrowing down the work to the bare essentials with stretched resources and chipping away at so called non-essentials. Instead, we need for boards to embrace both the 'meaningful outside' – seeking out ideas and partnerships in order to inspire a 'bottom-up' tide of innovative approaches to managing sustainability. It also requires boards to maintain a focus on the legacy mindset – namely how they prepare their organisations to adapt, survive and thrive in a challenging future. A board that doesn't possess the legacy mindset may find their CEO becomes very reactive and short-termist in their approach to sustainability:

> 'First time CEOs rarely have much experience with weighing the balance toward a long-term future [...]. Typically they've been accountable for results only a few months ahead [...]. Their instincts for investing for long-term have not been honed. Those instincts often arise from on-the-job training.' – A. Lafley, CEO of Procter and Gamble, Harvard Business Review.

As we have seen elsewhere, the mindset the board creates pervades the organisation. In this case, the board will either be more inclined to an investor mindset or a bean counter mindset. An investor mindset will look at investing in the people, resources, models and relationships that will set the organisation for overcoming tighter funding and improving services in the process. The bean counter mindset will instead look at the ever-diminishing pot of money that comes into the bank every year and ask 'what can we cut first?' The bean counters will often seek to reduce the back office first (the place where the investors generate the leadership and project management of innovative delivery models); they will cut some services that, whilst not essential, have an indirect positive impact on the frontline and foster innovation; and they will push suppliers and contractors to the limits of patience, in their pursuit of lower fees. Quality is hit as a result.

Sir John Jones talks about poverty thinkers, probability thinkers, and possibility thinkers. Many organisations – including multi-academy trusts – must move away from poverty thinking, which corrodes an organisation and its peoples' ability to think out of the box, and be creative and optimistic (as far as possible) in response to what are significant sustainability challenges. That's easier said than done, but it will define the success of organisations and their CEOs in the coming years.

Bean counters or investors?

Bean counters:

- See 'the budget' as the limit of resource available.
- See the budget as something to be spent rather than to be invested strategically.
- Look to cut 'non-essentials' first rather than reforming both non-essential and essentials.
- Maintain the same old ways of engaging suppliers and undertaking delivery – just try to get it for less!
- Resist taking risks in investing in new models of delivery.
- See the budget as 'king'; strategy must fall in line with it.

Investors:

- See the budget as the beginning; look at how they cannot only spend it efficiently but invest it wisely'.
- Look to wider sources of funding and grant opportunities; consider how improving services also provides opportunities for income generation.
- Invest in people and delivery models that are – in the long-term – more efficient and lead to improvements.
- Look outwards to organisations with common goals to find collaborative approaches to delivery and income generation.
- See the budget as the servant of the organisation's strategy.

The bean counters are intensely focused on 'the business we are in' and protecting core delivery at the expense of everything else that in the long run supports it. The 'meaningful outside' – a place of austerity – must be the wolf that is kept from the door. They hunker down and keep cutting and reducing. They will often avoid asking hard questions about the frontline – regarding it as sacred and immune from reform, whilst cutting the sources from which they will gather innovation and reform. They are also intensely focused on short-term results, making sure budgets stack up as they were intended to. The legacy mindset and the focus on embracing the opportunities and learning that exist in 'the meaningful outside' are overlooked.

It is perhaps counter-intuitive for some CEOS to embrace the ambiguity and certain degree of risk the investor mindset entails; however, the only certainty of cutting back to core and failing to invest is reduced services and greater risk to delivery. The best CEOs weigh up the two roads they can take – and they set off with the right group of people joining them on the journey.

The growing premium on entrepreneurial leadership

With the backing of the board, the CEO must recognise the huge importance of translating strategy into operational delivery – and, as with driving delivery and improvement, the CEO can't address this challenge alone. They need a senior team that can rise to the challenge, with the right mindset for addressing the sustainability and growth challenges head on, whilst also ensuring everything the organisation does is aligned to its vision and values.

This is where, in my view, entrepreneurial leadership is now at a premium. In some sectors, especially the public sector, entrepreneurialism is considered to be a dirty word. It is considered by some to sully the standing of long-standing professions, or, worse, to wrongly imply that corporate masters are treating sacred public-funded organisations like profit-making enterprises. We must get over this. And, not only must we get over this, we must build the capability of our organisations to embrace it so that we can meet the very real challenge set out by ACEVO of a context where there is both reduced funding and greater demand on services.

The reality is that entrepreneurial zeal in both the public and charities sector is now a moral imperative – not simply because of the funding challenges and the need to overcome them, but also because of the need to address the complex challenges of the world around us with innovative ways of delivering services that ensure our organisations remain relevant. More than ever, CEOs need to be demonstrating and encouraging values-driven, entrepreneurial leadership on their teams.

However, too often, CEOs can find themselves struggling to find this entrepreneurial zeal in teams of highly qualified people – the long-time experts and the specialists. The specialist advice they can receive is second to none, but in my experience, some CEOs are all too often alone in taking an 'organisation-wide' strategic view of resourcing and investment that looks at how the organisation prioritises its investments, resourcing, and seeks to deliver new ways of working.

This is so important, because – as we saw with achieving improvement and innovation at scale in Chapter 6 – the CEO is not in a position to deliver the all-important entrepreneurial bridge between strategy and operational delivery. It is this task that I consider to best fit the description of Deputy CEO and in specialist improvement organisations like a multi-academy trust, the CEO (who is often a specialist) needs someone expert in organisational development to perform that role.

How does this apply to multi-academy trusts?

In the multi-academy trust sector, the general consensus is that in building a central team the role of finance director must come first. Some trust CEOs have taken this to the letter, at the detriment – in my view at least – to ensuring the organisation becomes genuinely strategic about investing in its long-term growth and development.

I believe that the role of Chief Finance Officer (CFO) or Finance Director is an essential one – every organisation needs this input, advice and planning at a very senior level. However, unlike a Chief Operating Officer (COO), the finance role is one that tends to lean towards financial budgeting process and audit; rather than strategic investment and resourcing and operational innovation. This is an important distinction when we consider organisational sustainability. Budgeting and robust financial processes are one (crucial) element of the organisation's responsibilities – making sure that money is allocated to where there is most need, that it is spent wisely, and that any risk of underspend or overspend is managed.

Strategic investment and resourcing, however, is an all-pervading role – and one that is absolutely essential to getting the sustainability issue (and successful organisational growth) right. In most MATs, what a CEO needs on a day-to-day basis is a second-in command who can provide sufficient financial oversight, but also complement the CEO in terms of securing strong operational leadership across the board in areas beyond school improvement (assuming the CEO is of a school improvement background). It is these areas that some MATs are more likely to cut than reform in their quest for sustainability.

The crucial appointment of the Chief Operating Officer

This second-in-command role is an important appointment for any CEO. I think some CEOs are taking this decision too lightly, from a position of fear and a lack of confidence, rather than a position of humility and strategic foresight.

A number of CEOs are tempted to appoint someone internally, which usually means promote – again, often from a finance background. It's tempting because it's usually cheaper that way and the relationship is already well established. The CEO believes that they should hold onto the organisational strategy for themselves – appointing someone from an accountancy or financial management background (or a business manager). They are driven to do this because they feel the need – through a lack of confidence – to plug an operational gap in their thinking and knowledge; that lack of confidence trumps a focus on enhancing the strategic leadership of their organisation. Unfortunately, this approach too often fails and leaves the CEO struggling and isolated, because they have failed to create a role that can 'bridge the gap' between strategy and operations.

Not so far into growth, most MAT CEOs realise they actually need someone befitting the role of Chief Operating Officer – ensuring that finances, resourcing, procurement, technology, risk management and operating processes neatly dovetail together to help deliver the organisational vision and achieve sustainability. Far from being simply about finance, the COO role 'defies a one-size fits all description [...]. It is a job whose responsibilities are defined closely in tandem with the individual needs and goals of the chief executive officer'. Furthermore, the COO is 'a breed of executive who combines deep operational knowledge with broad strategic insight'. (EY, The DNA of the COO, 2012). Balancing the books and ensuring financial compliance is essential work in this climate, but – as a standalone skill set – it doesn't get anywhere near to what a CEO of a growing or a large trust needs in terms of operational leadership.

It is my view that the CEO must always appoint someone who can support and challenge their thinking on a strategic level and translate it – with an entrepreneurial mindset – into action, helping them to maximise all resources across the organisation in order to deliver the vision. The finance director or COO who cannot do that will be a liability for a CEO – particularly in today's climate. This is because, as Joe Trammel (author of the CEO tightrope) puts it, too many organisations fall into the trap where too 'often management action is driven by budgets and the budgeting process'. This is a real danger in an age of austerity, because the organisation's resources and services quickly begin to be driven by the budgets, rather than served by them.

A CEO and a board may wish to pursue sustainable models of resourcing and delivery, but a finance director, without adequate strategic insight or oversight across the organisation, can quickly become the blocker and the wider long-term vision for sustainability fails to translate into decision making at all levels of the organisation. The budget itself becomes king. In these circumstances – despite the best intentions of the board and the CEO – a bean counting mindset trumps an investor and entrepreneurial mindset. Many MATs are already falling into that trap, as the budgets get tighter.

The characteristics of a strong COO

In appointing a Chief Operating Officer, experienced COO and CEO Caroline Maley (now Chair of an NHS healthcare trust) says CEOs and boards must have reference to the fact that: 'a core skill of the COO/CFO is their ability to bring out the best in people. They must also have a good understanding of how businesses work, the ability to work across a wide range of areas and to manage teams of skilled people. MATs are multi-million pound businesses so having access to a really good COO is vital.' This is supported by a thinkpiece by EY, 'The DNA of the COO',[45] which states: 'COO responsibilities differ, but one theme remains constant. To perform the role well, 87% of COOs say that highly developed leadership qualities and interpersonal skills are the most crucial attributes.'

Indeed, the CEO usually needs someone who can help them deliver the vision in challenging circumstances, whilst also being ready to challenge and bring to bear expertise around what is possible and what is not. In *Rocket Fuel: The One Essential Combination That Will Get You More of What You Want from Your Business* by Gino Wickman and Mark C. Winters, the authors describe the importance of having people at the top of an organisation who provide the 'visionary' and the 'integrator' elements. Whilst it is important that the COO is strategic, they must be able to integrate all aspects of the business – the resources, the delivery, the external relationships, and the financing – through a sustainable business plan, so that vision becomes a reality.

This is why the relationship matters so much and that the skills sets and experiences of the CEO and COO complement each other well. The honest truth is that many CEOs in the public sector do not have a career history that has encouraged them to develop the entrepreneurial experience to translate vision into operations in a way that breeds sustainability through successful strategic integration at scale. There are exceptions, but humble, learning CEOs who are alive to the challenges around them will spot the gap and fill it.

Harvard Business Review published an article in 2006 (Second in Command)[46] on what it considered to be, as a result of its research,

45. EY. (No date) 'The DNA of the COO: Time to claim the spotlight'. Available at: www.ey.com/publication/vwluassetspi/the_dna_of_the_coo_-_time_to_claim_ the_spotlight/$file/dna%20of%20the%20coo.pdf

46. Bennett, N & Miles, S, A. (2006) 'Second in Command: The Misunderstood Role of the Chief Operating Officer'. (Harvard Business Review) Available at: https://hbr.org/2006/05/second-in-command-the-misunderstood-role-of-the-chief-operating-officer

the seven kinds of COO. These were: Executor (delivering on behalf the CEO), Mentor (to a new or inexperienced CEO), Change Agent (delivering organisational reform and new ways of working), Heir Apparent (the COO that is being groomed to take on the CEO role next), the Partner or Other Half, and the MVP (most valued person that the organisation doesn't wish to lose, so it promotes them to COO!).

Certainly the COO of a MAT needs to have the skills, experience and competencies to complement a CEO who – for the most part – will be very new to the job, very much needing to drive change in response to the complexity and sustainability issues raised in this chapter, and very much in need of someone who can deliver (execute) operationally in response to that complexity and a tight financial climate. The choice of COO cannot be underestimated. I would also go so far to say that a good COO in a MAT would increasingly be in a strong position to take on the ultimate strategic leadership of those organisations in the years to come.

Yet it's a challenging task to recruit the right person; it requires careful time and thought. The same Harvard Business Review article stated that 'the tremendous variation in COO roles and responsibilities manifestly implies that there is no standard set of 'great COO' attributes. This makes finding suitable candidates difficult for executive recruiters. More important, it stymies the CEOs and boards who must select among the candidates. The existence of seven different roles suggests at least seven different sets of attributes on top of the basic – and infinitely variable – requirement that there exist a personal chemistry between the COO and the current CEO.'

Indeed, it goes without saying that the relationship must be based on trust, honesty, frankness, mutual understanding, professional respect, and a 'can do' mindset. There must also be that personal chemistry. The desired outcome of this is an on-going dialogue that ensures the use of resources is prioritised and maximised, whilst also sometimes – in these challenging times – finding creative and legitimate ways to make crucial things happen without the cash or internal people to do it. For example, through fundraising, corporate social responsibility schemes, or engaging volunteers.

A COO with experience of growing a business to scale, of delivering efficient scalable systems that maximise the organisation's resources and external relationships, and of fundraising and generating social capital through volunteerism, is a huge asset to multi-academy trusts in the current context. A good COO will have experience of leading at least some of these crucial strategies. It will be challenging for a CEO to find a CFO who can provide this crucial bridge between strategy and operational leadership.

What should CEOs consider when pursuing sustainable development?

So, in their quest for sustainability, where should CEOs and their COOs begin? The answer to this is almost always the customer/end user experience. This is the ultimate way in which an organisation's success is determined, and, therefore, whether it has achieved successful and sustainable growth. In MATs, ensuring the most enriching and engaging educational experience for all pupils is the fundamental purpose. CEOs should begin with their vision for the curriculum and vision for learning and educational experiences and ask, 'what resources do we need to do to make it happen?' This should be considered by looking forward over a number of years – with a view to developing talent internally, building school improvement expertise, and accessing resources and contributions from beyond the MAT through strategic partnerships.

The finance director or COO's job is then to ensure – in partnership with senior leaders and teachers – that the resources are delivered, but also to develop the strategic partnerships between schools and with other organisations to maximise resource and talent. Who from within and beyond the organisation can contribute to delivery of the highest standards, and how can we ensure it represents value? In my view, there should be no compromise on this front. An organisation must be 'self-sustaining' in its core work.

The second area where little compromise should be taken is on recruitment and retention of the very best staff. The quality of teachers and support staff is the area of greater influence on the MAT's core business – giving children and young people the best start and ensuring they achieve strong outcomes. Indeed, investing in becoming 'employer of choice' can reap dividends. The amounts some trusts spend on recruitment advertising and supply – even in this climate – are eye watering. If trusts can invest in areas that employees are increasingly prioritising – such as the professional development, wellbeing, mentoring and coaching, and strategies to mitigate the workload of staff, they will reap the long-term rewards of retaining the best and having a reputation as an employer that goes before it. A CEO that invests in people will save a fortune in the long run.

A number of MATs are now also investing strategically in their own supply banks, ensuring that supply teachers are quality assured and trained, without paying excessive fees both for supply and to convert supply teachers into full time employees. It should also not be forgotten that investing in the training and development of trustees and governors, as well as leaders, is crucial, not least for the purposes of compliance. So many examples of fundamental MAT failure are down to a lack of training for people in these roles.

Economies of scale

So that leaves the rest, areas to save money and cut costs or areas to work strategically and invest? Across so many elements of a trust's work, there is the opportunity to achieve economies of scale. This can be achieved through avoiding duplications of roles across the organisation, where central support and better systems and processes can just as easily serve the same purpose. This is where a Chief Operating Officer role comes into its own, because this is all about redesigning and remodelling services so that, whilst duplication can be avoided, those central services and processes continue to meet the needs of the separate facets of the organisation with the same level of responsiveness and to even higher standards.

Economies of scale can also be achieved by auditing contracts entered into by different sites and asking, 'will we achieve better economies by procuring these services together rather than separately?' There will be times when cross-trust or organisational-wide procurement is not suitable, however a good COO and their team will look wherever possible to procure at scale whilst working with individual schools or branches to develop separate service level agreements to meet local need. This, again, is about understanding delivery models as well as the financial aspects – ensuring services are not only accessed at good value, but also in a way that maintains and ensures organisational success.

Another way in which economies of scale can be readily achieved is through undertaking talent audits of staff at all levels. This is another example of where the interdependency of HR leadership, procurement, and finance all marry together. If an organisation truly understands the skills, qualifications and experiences of its workforce, it can begin to harness those in a way that recognises people's talents and contributions whilst also achieving sustainability. For example, I know of one academy trust that audited the skills of its site managers across schools. In doing so, it identified one with significant experience as a plumber, another with experience of working with heating systems and boilers, and another with experience of joinery. Together, they have pooled those experiences across schools to address the costs of boiler maintenance and the building of new playground equipment – saving tens of thousands of pounds.

Another trust found through talent audit that one of its site managers had been an electrician (long forgotten by the management who had not originally recruited the individual), and are now putting this individual through PAT testing qualifications to save the trust thousands of pounds a year across its multiple sites. Other examples in trusts are those that have identified musicians, accountants, tree surgeons, plasterers and bid writers in their ranks – and have recognised the enormous savings and (crucially) benefits to service that could be achieved by harnessing this untapped resource. A good, entrepreneurial CEO that understands the interplay between HR, finance, and service delivery, will invest in the talent and people that already exist within the organisation first in order to achieve savings, improved services, and sustainability. Once that has been exhausted, an organisation should seek to develop strategic, supportive, and aligned partnerships with other organisations that can help us in our quest for sustainability. The strength of those partnerships almost always begin with the CEO.

Partnerships for sustainability

The pursuit of economies of scale has limitations. However large an organisation becomes, it will need to draw on expertise, skills and capacity of others beyond it. There will always be limitations to what you can do with internal resource. I will consider the importance of social and professional capital in Chapter 8, however it is worth looking at it in relation to sustainability at this juncture.

CEOs should invest time developing relationships with their top suppliers so that suppliers are invested in the partnership and are ready to provide a responsive service and 'go the extra mile'. This is an often overlooked feature of the CEO role, with leadership books often focusing in on the importance of meeting the needs of the 'customer' or end user and ensuring staff are motivated and supported in their work.

However, in a highly interdependent and complex world, the services we provide – be it an enriching curriculum and learning environment, or otherwise – also fundamentally depend on having motivated and engaged suppliers who care deeply about providing the very best possible service. The problem is, again, that if finance people are responsible for the relationship with suppliers, those relationships are very much focused, understandably, on getting the best bang for buck, rather than nurturing quality and goodwill.

I recognise that may be a sweeping statement, but as a CEO and supplier to many organisations myself, I know how all too often that engagement with finance teams within our client organisations can be very much about the money and the process of the transaction, rather than an interest in the service offered or the importance of building a mutually-beneficial relationship over time. This matters enormously. If your 'supplier facing' team are almost entirely focused on budgets and securing the best bang for buck, a supplier can readily lose their sense of purpose in the partnership, their emotional investment in it, and – yes – the element of discretionary effort. What arises is a transactional relationship that people do not feel invested in and where 'getting the best' deal matters to both sides. Losing that is a big issue in an era where sustainability and value for money matters more than ever.

CEOs are in a unique position to set the tone, recognising their suppliers by meeting with them once in a while, getting their feedback on how things are going, and, if things are going well, sending the odd note of gratitude and expressing the difference that the 'partnership' means to them. A COO is in a good position to maintain that relationship on a week-to-week basis, ensuring that the supplier is valued and that – operationally – things are managed as well as possible so that both sides are able to do their job to the best of their ability.

An organisation that sees its suppliers as partners will reap the benefits of goodwill, good customer service, and a deep commitment to high quality service over the long-term. That is a very sustainable way of doing business.

Related to this is the partnership with volunteers. For many charitable and public service organisations, volunteerism has always been essential to their important work and their ability to deliver. This is something that has not been tapped into to the same scale by trusts and schools, yet – if they are to succeed in the years of austerity and complexity ahead – it will become essential. This will be on the radar of every forward thinking academy trust CEO. As we have seen in Chapter 3, leadership narrative is essential to drawing in volunteers who can add both social and professional capital to the work of trusts. Yet something else is needed. David Strudley CBE, former CEO of Acorns and Rainbows Children's Hospice, is a CEO who knows the value of volunteerism. The two organisations he led depended on their commitment, generosity and talents to deliver.

Like I have suggested with suppliers, David suggests that volunteers must be made to feel an essential part of the organisation, with their roles recognised and celebrated. Not only must they feel cared for, they must also feel 'loved'. As David says 'love 'em'![47] That's not to say expectations should be compromised. But, as CEO, if you start from a position where you 'love' your suppliers and your volunteers, the benefits to organisational sustainability and success can be enormous. As David and so many other leaders leading organisations experiencing austerity have found.

---

47. Forum Strategy. (2018) *Leaders In Conversation: Episode 2 – David Strudley CBE*
[Video] Available at: www.youtube.com/watch?v=Scr3AArGaTE

Collaborating with peer organisations

Another important partnership for organisations, and particularly for academy trusts, is the relationship with their peers. Some will look at their peers purely as competitors, others will see them as collaborators and as a source of support and mutual-benefit. In the pursuit of sustainability, we are strongly encouraging MATs to think about how they can collaborate on some back office services rather than reinvent the wheel across multiple trusts. There are some CEOs that are already looking at this – considering strategic partnerships with other MATs on areas such as shared leadership roles, shared professional development, educational psychology services, staff supply banks, catering services, and more, but for more examples please see Appendix 4.

This is an important avenue to pursue (with strong reference to the board); because it provides an opportunity to deliver services together – better, cheaper and all the time enhancing pupils' learning and healthy development. However, it requires a genuine commitment to building deep collaborative partnerships with other trusts and an entrepreneurial mindset from both the CEO and the COO.

Careful growth

Another important priority for CEOs must be due-diligence and as a recent report stated, this should be 'a comprehensive process including not only financial and teaching, but also estate management, human resources and procurement'. A CEO that is so focused on growth can easily fall into a trap, as decisions are made without sufficient consideration of the impact that a new school will have on the organisation's finances or capacity. A good COO will understand the lie of the land here, and be able to bring to bear a deep understanding of those areas that do not reflect the CEO's experience and expertise. That is why it is so important that the CEO and COOs skills' sets complement one another. Too many trusts have failed because the quest for growth (and a confidence about delivering one particular area – school improvement) trumped the need to ensure overall sustainability and viability.

Compliance

Which leaves us with compliance. Compliance begins with governance, and this continues to prove to be a major stumbling block for the academy trust sector. Too many trustees have struggled to make the transition from governors to trustees and to fully grasp their responsibilities in company law, charity law, and to one another. This is a big risk; the CEO and members need a trust board that is ready and well placed to hold the organisation to account, fully appraised of the duties that need to be discharged and the statutory framework within which their organisations work.

As with the employer of choice agenda, it cannot be over emphasised how important it is for the trustees to be well inducted and training (with access to on-going training and resources as legislation and regulations change). We still come across few trusts that have a compliance register, detailing all the organisation's responsibilities and duties, who is responsible for them, and their status in terms of whether and how they have been discharged. This is not a risk register; it is more encompassing.

It's critical that the board has faith in staff that discharge many of the statutory duties and other responsibilities. The CEO as accounting officer is the bridge here, and must ensure that there are adequate systems and processes in place for ensuring duties and responsibilities are not only discharged at all levels of the organisation, but that the board and executive team can be clear about who is responsible, whether they have discharged their duties, and any risks or issues that may stand in the way of those duties being discharged. In a large organisation, having a compliance register as well as a risk register is essential for good governance. By having these systems and processes in place, the board and its committees, as well as the CEO and executive team, can adequately monitor compliance and – if necessary – 'deep dive' into areas where potential issues and risk lie.

In that vein, one way in which the time, commitment and focus can be given to ensuring compliance is through an effective committee structure, whereby trustees with more in-depth expertise and knowledge of a given area – be it finance or otherwise, can provide strong oversight and scrutiny of executive leaders. The CEO should encourage this and should encourage their team to engage fully and properly with the challenge and accountability it brings. Meanwhile, it must also be said that a board cannot delegate their overall responsibilities and duties to others – including financial and as an employer, so ensuring that the reporting and remit of a committee is clear and well understood by the board, as a whole, is crucial.

A CEO needs to have confidence in their board and in the processes, and, whilst they shouldn't be managing their board or involving themselves in the boards' development, the CEO (in partnership with the COO and chair) can make a big contribution toward ensuring the board is developing the capacity and processes for ensuring compliance. This is one of the reasons that I believe the CEO's membership of a board is so important, because they must have that sense of partnership and shared responsibility in discharging the organisation's duty to be compliant. Their expertise and their oversight of day-to-day operations is a key factor in ensuring the board achieves compliance.

Questions for reflection

- Do you have the board's backing to pursue an 'investor' approach to sustainability? As an organisation, can you take an entrepreneurial approach to some aspects of delivery in order to achieve new efficiencies and better services, not least through investing in new resources and partnerships up front?

- Do you have access to experienced organisational development and delivery leadership – often found through an experienced COO – who can help you translate your sustainability strategy into the organisation's delivery models?

- Is the organisation adequately maximising its internal resource through 'habit' and is this resource deployed as effectively as possible?

- Are your relationships with other MATs giving rise to strategic sharing of resources (even if with a commercial element to the relationship) and some joint procurement, helping to save money and improve quality?

Chapter 8

Fostering key relationships, building social and professional capital

'Leadership was once about muscles, now
it's about getting along with people.'
- Gandhi

Many of our MAT Leaders members[48] have been picking up our
recommended reading, *New Power*, which considers the shift taking place
from leadership that is predicated on the power that comes with position
and money; to a new concept of leadership, where power is generated
from the 'bottom-up' and relies on networks, influence and social
capital. It's an exciting time to be a leader, a time of endless possibilities
unbound by the traditional structures and barriers of the past. However,
only some leaders are recognising the shift and the significant influence
it will have on their organisations in the decade ahead.

---

48. Forum Strategy. (No Date) 'Networks & Training'. Available at:
www.forumstrategy.org/contact/

In the book, they draw on the example of NASA. In 2010 the organisation faced the prospect of severe cuts by Congress (recognise this!). There was also a perception that the organisation was not being as innovative as it had been. NASA responded to these duel challenges – the need to balance budgets and the need to deliver new approaches – by instigating something that it called 'open innovation'. Rather than enlist a small group of internal experts to solve problems, open innovation draws people in from beyond the organisation who have a passion for the subject matter, knowledge on it, and relevant expertise. New York University professor Hila Lifshitz-Assaf followed NASA on its journey of open innovation for three years, undertaking an in-depth three-year longitudinal field study of the initiative.

NASA picked out fourteen strategic research and development challenges and opened them up for the world to take on and provide solutions. 3000 people replied, as Heiman and Timms tell us 'ranging from experts to unrecognised enthusiasts'. The impact of this open innovation was that problems were being solved within three to six months, rather than the usual three to five years the organisation had traditionally taken on comparable challenges. As Heiman and Timms say, 'not only did the crowd produce quicker solutions, at much lower cost, the quality of its work was significantly higher than expected.' One particular issue that 'the crowd' addressed was a serious problem in heliophysics: the challenge of predicting solar storms. Bruce Cragin, a semi-retired telecommunications engineer from New Hampshire submitted an algorithm that trebled the time within which solar storms have traditionally been forecast by NASA to eight hours, and improved the level of accuracy from 50% to 75%. And he wasn't even an expert in heliophysics!

There were two polar opposite responses to the rise of 'open innovation' and Heiman and Timms describe the division that arose as a result of this. Whilst one camp embraced it with enthusiasm, another saw it as a waste of time, then, as it gained traction, a threat. Whilst some professionals within NASA resisted the sharing of information and lamented the budgets being spent on open innovation, others threw themselves into designing new processes and models for further encouraging open innovation – with some employees even leaving the organisation to help set up a new unit called 'open NASA'.

There was clearly a proprietary mindset emerging. Those who resisted the emergence of open innovation were observed in meetings brandishing their CVs and regularly referring to their extensive professional qualifications. Some went as far as to deride the inputs of those who came in from beyond the organisation and the direct professional spheres that the strategic research areas covered.

The problem is that this proprietorial resistance amongst some professionals and others is increasingly – as we see with NASA – going against the grain of a high interconnected, technologically driven world where the 'wisdom of the crowd' (and capacity of the crowd, I would add) represents enormous potential value to any organisation. This is particularly true, as we saw with NASA, where there are tightening budgets and expanding challenges! It is the role of the CEO, as the person who sets the leadership narrative of the organisation, sets the tone for the culture of the organisation, and who enables the pillars of improvement at scale, to help their organisations make this transition from old power to new power. As we have seen so often in this book, this is about a new era of professional and organisational humility, and recognising that the world is becoming – for many reasons – far more interdependent.

This notion of drawing upon the social and professional capital that exists beyond our organisations is a fascinating idea and one that is beginning to play out in our education system, not least in an age of technological upheaval combined with austerity and the increasingly complex challenges (and opportunities) facing children and young people. Trusts and schools simply cannot rely on their own people and capacity to shape the ambitious visions that respond to this turbulent context. Leadership needs to evolve as a result.

How does this apply to multi-academy trusts?

The success of our end-users (children and young people) now fundamentally depends on a number of things, not least providing them with a secure platform for healthy development and their ability to use technology as a force for good. Yet, what we see instead is a generation of children whose life satisfaction is amongst the lowest in the developed world; declining mental health; the all-pervading influence of the internet and AI creating a chasm between 'masters' and 'servants' of technology; and the lowest levels of time spent outdoors than any other previous generation – impacting on physical health. Couple that with new models of employment – including growing self-employment – that bring opportunity for huge flexibility and creativity, but also uncertainty and a lack of safeguards for the next generation of workers (today's pupils).

When we discuss these issues with CEOs and heads, we are met with a deep sense of frustration – not only based on the fact that children and young people are facing these challenges, but also that funding is limited and that there simply isn't enough time in the day to address all of them alone. So many of the initiatives announced by government in response are piecemeal and limited in scope. It appears that, at least in providing a strategic response, leaders are on their own.

Yet, they aren't. Only those waiting for national strategies from government are. Because what all of this represents is a need for CEOs and leaders – using their ever-growing influence and scale through multi-academy trusts – to develop 'new power' and work towards developing the networks and social capital that can help them develop a generation of confident, happy and successful young people. Indeed, it's the only choice. Drawing on the time, expertise and resources of others – beyond the education system – is going to be key. As Gandhi said, leadership is no longer about muscles, it is about getting along with people. The CEO's narrative and the relationships they forge are just as powerful as the money, position or traditional levers. The most successful leaders of the next decade will recognise their role in fostering social capital.

What does this look like in practice? Well, it requires academy CEOs and trust boards to step up to a new leadership plate – and, like NASA, to open up the relationships with communities, businesses, charities and higher education framed within their narrative for giving their pupils the very best start. This is both necessary and enormously exciting for this generation of leaders. It is the calling of MAT leaders, given their influence and scale, to be the guardians and champions of young people

– providing the leadership narrative (as we saw in Chapter 3) that others, within and beyond the organisation collaborate around.

These external relationships are likely to be diverse, but all – if they are to have traction – will need to be framed within a compelling narrative for ensuring this generation of pupils thrive, in the face of the challenges and opportunities they face. These relationships – depending on context – could involve:

- Working with cutting-edge technology companies in shaping the learning experiences of pupils, not least in understanding how tech can be a force for good and enrich people's lives and society as a whole;

- Working in partnership with local sports clubs and environmental groups to enthuse young people to put down the tech and engage in inspiring physical and outdoors activity;

- Developing relationships with local voluntary organisations – also in need of help in tight financial times – to ensure pupils develop a sense of place and social responsibility, in an age of superficial online relationships;

- Engaging with regional businesses so that trusts and their schools can benefit from corporate social responsibility funding and initiatives;

- Engaging with higher education, not simply for teacher training purposes but to draw on the wealth of specialist talent amongst lecturers and academics, and opportunities to access resources. Remember, HEI needs a 'shop window' to your young people;

- Developing relationships with the early years sector to share intelligence, best practice and resources. They are your future pupils;

- Working across multi-academy trusts to share expertise and resources – drawing on one another's specific strengths;

- Drawing on the knowledge and skills of young people themselves to mentor one another, and provide supportive relationships, perhaps across the boundaries of communities and academy trusts.

At our recent #MATLeaders conference, I described CEOs as being '**the conductor of the orchestra**'. A key role in being the conductor is to understand which external relationships are going to enhance and enrich the curriculum and the learning experiences of children and young people, as well as ensure their healthy development. This is about much more than dealing with the politics and civil servants.

Every MAT should have a 'living' list of key stakeholders, and a clear view of why that organisation or person is a key stakeholder and what it is that the relationship should try to achieve. The challenge here is really knowing which relationships to forge!

Collaborating strategically and avoiding collaborative overload

As with sustainability, the starting point has to be the vision for the organisation, based – as we have seen – on clarity around the business we are in, our interpretation of the meaningful outside, and a legacy mindset. If we don't have a clear view of the vision, then it is difficult to know which relationships will align with it and truly add value, and which will lead to excessive and undisciplined collaboration – something that is often described as 'collaborative overload'.

According to Rob Cross, a professor of global leadership at Babson College, 'The collaborative intensity of work has exploded over the past decade.'[49] He says, as I highlighted earlier in this chapter, that this is driven by the growing complexity of work and the increasing interdependencies that creates. In research for his 2016 article for Harvard Business Review, Cross – together with colleagues – found that 'the time spent by managers and employees in collaborative activities has ballooned by 50% or more'. Organisations experiencing collaborative overload soon feel the strain, and according to Cross et al 'performance suffers as (staff) are buried under an avalanche of requests for input or advice, access to resources, or attendance at a meeting. They take assignments home, and soon, according to a large body of evidence on stress, burnout and turnover become real risks.'

49. Cross, R. (9 November 2017) 'Too Much Togetherness? The Downside of Workplace Collaboration'. Available at: http://knowledge.wharton.upenn.edu/article/much-togetherness-downside-workplace-collaboration/

So how do organisations avoid becoming everything to everyone and engaging in multiple forms of collaboration that rather than add value, put the organisation at serious risk? Cross encourages leaders to pursue collaboration with reference to their 'North Star', only entering into partnerships and activities that contribute to their goals and not getting drawn into things where either they don't add unique value or that are not important to them.

Through a clear leadership narrative, others in the organisation should be encouraged to determine which partnerships and collaborative activity fits this description and which don't. One important way in which CEOs and organisations should embark on collaborative activity is by asking two sets of key questions with the potential partner:

- Where are we aligned in terms of our organisational vision, and what are the mutual-benefits of partnership? Do the benefits justify the time and energy that need to be invested in this relationship?
- Where is the potential for competition or conflict in this relationship? Does that competition of potential for conflict outweigh the benefits of collaboration?

Liz Richardson, a Senior Lecturer at the University of Manchester and co-author of the book *Nudge, Nudge, Think, Think* has developed a very useful model for how organisations, groups, and people come together to establish the basis for co-creation. She warns about organisations chasing what she calls 'policy unicorns' – wonderful ideas that actually are very challenging to pursue in practice. She recommends that organisations and groups come together with a 'compelling need', hence the importance of a leadership narrative, set by the CEO that seeks common ground, but that this is then put through a process of determining alignment:

Addition or subtraction? The benefits to both parties must be such that both are gaining a mutual benefit from the relationship. If one party is losing out, the relationship is unsustainable and lacks viability in the long run. Commitment will be lost if one party is gaining and the other isn't.

Art. Do both organisations share similar vision and values so that people come together with a genuine desire to support one another's work?

Craft. Are the day-to-day realities of both organisations' work such that they can readily work together in a practical way? An example of where this may not work is where an organisation is too geographically distant from another group, where lots of 'red tape' must be cut through in order to get projects off the ground, or where statutory duties conflict.

Science. Are the organisations and groups involved aligned in terms of the evidence base and the science behind the initiatives being undertaken? Do they have a shared sense of 'what works' and what needs to be done, or is there conflict around how services are delivered?

If these 'gateways' to collaborative working and co-creation of services can be overcome this means unearthing the potential for conflict and competition and seeing if this is surmountable. It also means determining that genuine commitment to mutual benefit exists on both sides.

Kate Lester, CEO of Diamond Logistics and a multi-award winning entrepreneur, running one of country's 100 fastest growing companies, has the following view: 'I think the essence of a good partnership versus a bad partnership is that you each of equal 'skin in the game' and that it is mutually beneficial [...]. There is nothing as pointless as having a partnership where what drives everyone is what he or she can take from the relationship; the partnership has to be about what you think you can give. Ultimately speaking – if you are looking at a commercial contract – there will be an element of that; but when it comes to shared social or professional endeavours – there isn't room for that! In order to get it right, leave egos at the door, have equal skin in the game, and choose your partners as carefully as you choose your clients, your franchises and your employees – it has to be a good fit, have a slow courtship!'[50]

Indeed, Liz Richardson describes how organisations should go about 'releasing the beasts'. This means working within a shared set of protocols or understandings that give rise to true collaboration and co-creation that realise the benefits of social and professional capital. These are:

---

50. Forum Strategy. (15 December 2018) 'Leaders In Conversation – Episoder 3'. [Video] Available at: www.youtube.com/watch?v=dDeswJYrqrE

- Transparent values: maintaining clarity on the motivations for entering into the partnership.

- Engaged: a commitment to the partnership and not neglecting the time and effort required.

- Respect for expertise: leaving egos at the door and respecting all colleagues, whatever their position, for what they bring to the table.

- Relational: investing time and effort in relationships and understanding each other's perspectives.

- Asset-based: ensuring that genuine resource is shared.

- Positive-sum: recognising that generosity of spirit and 'giving' leads to returns; not constantly asking 'what do we get from this?' or seeking a quid pro quo.

- Iterative: knowing that each step will take time, and must be decided and determined in conjunction, based on evidence, reflection, and reference to the 'end user'.

- Not decided in advance: ensuring that one party does not come in with a specific agenda that is to the detriment of others in the relationship.

- Self-aware: again, leaving egos at the door and recognising oneself as a partner in the process, not a manager of it.

Again, humility plays an enormous role in all of this. The CEO sets the tone because it is they that will initiate and nurture the strategic partnerships and collaborative ventures. Going into these 'social capital' partnerships with a sense of parity, of respect, and a genuine desire to find common ground and mutual-benefit.

However, that must constantly be balanced with an assessment of the value of the partnership and how it continues to align with and support the goals of the organisation. As conductor of the orchestra, the CEO must be confident that the partnership will be of sufficient value and not lead the organisation and its people further into collaborative overload. This is because our organisations only have finite time and resource to invest in maintaining and following through the partnerships we embark on.

The role of the board

MAT CEOs should also consider how they could be helped and supported in their efforts to foster a sense of mutual-benefit with key partners. The trust board should also understand its responsibilities here, not only in championing the vision externally, but also in drawing on their networks and relationships to draw on a wide-range of stakeholders who can each play a part in enhancing the development and learning of young people. We strongly welcome the recommendation of the NGA, that stakeholder engagement should be a fourth responsibility of governing boards.

How does the CEO approach this?

So, what tips do we have for CEOs looking to develop new power and ensure their organisations benefit from high social capital?

1. **Engage your trust board on the importance of external relationships.** Make the success of your chosen external relationships and how they benefit children and young people's lives a KPI for organisational success. Make sure you and the organisation are accountable for getting this right;

2. **Be clear on the leadership narrative and ensure it is compelling enough to bring people with you.** Communicate, communicate, communicate and seek areas for alignment with others. This is about securing the health and prosperity of the next generation – everyone cares about that!

3. **Get out there and tell the story!** Make a list – with your board and team – of organisations that can help to enhance children's learning and development; either through broader opportunities, professional expertise, resource and money, or otherwise. Use the media, local networking events, and the internet to make those important links.

4. **Ensure partnerships are entered into through the 'gateways' of shared 'art', craft and science.** Ensure each partner has equal 'skin in the game' and that the protocols of behaviour and activity are conducive to good partnership – including respect, self-awareness, commitment, generosity, and openness to ideas.

5. **Make it a reality for staff too.** You must tell the story and foster the relationships, but staff must deliver on it. The CEO is the champion and the prime networker – but you'll be overwhelmed if it's your responsibility to manage the relationships. CEOs that invest time and energy building social capital also risk collaborative overload.[51] Distribute responsibility to your staff (or board members) to manage the day-to-day relationships. This generation of graduates are particularly inspired to join organisations that are well connected and purposefully collaborate with others around a vision for change.

6. **Measure success.** Be clear about the impact that the relationship is having and if it is contributing to your vision for giving children that healthy and inspiring start to their lives. Survey stakeholders, pupils and staff for their views. Spend time on the relationships that add value, don't waste time on those that don't!

7. **Involve stakeholders in your visioning and strategic planning.** When we undertake visioning sessions with MATs, we actively encourage them to invite local stakeholders – including business and community groups. The potential for galvanising social capital often proves to be enormous. When that's done, create a advisory group for those external stakeholders who can add real value to your strategic development, and maybe recruit some of them to the trust board in the process!

Managing relationships with politicians and civil servants

For leaders of public sector organisations, politics and dealing with politicians and civil servants is an inevitable part of the role. Not only are changes in legislation, funding and other regulatory developments of concern to a CEO, but so too is the importance of maintaining politicians' and senior civil servants' confidence in organisations that deliver public services, which spend many millions of pounds and impact upon the lives of thousands of people. In the academy trust sector, trusts must maintain the confidence of RSCs (Regional Schools Commissioners)

---

51. Cross, R, Rebele, R & Grant, A. (2016) 'Collaborative Overload' (Harvard Business Review) Available at: www.hbr.org/2016/01/collaborative-overload

who are senior civil servants with responsibility across a number of key areas, not least for monitoring the performance of academy trusts, intervening where challenges are identified, and approving the on-going growth and development of trusts.

A CEO cannot avoid the importance of these crucial relationships. Without becoming consumed by them or distracted by how they are perceived by civil servants – remember, our end users are our 'market', this is the 'weather' – CEOs should invest a suitable amount of time in keeping key civil servants and politicians informed of developments, providing sufficient exposure to the work of the trust/organisation, and maintaining a productive professional relationship ready for when issues and opportunities that have a bearing on the trust and its pupils arise.

How do CEOs approach this? One important thing to remember is that senior politicians and civil servants have a substantial number of constituents and stakeholders. The demands on their time are significant. In working with a number of senior politicians in my time, I know how important it is that communications with them meet a number of criteria. Do not assume that just because you are the CEO that your communication or meeting will be prioritised at this level. I know some CEOs who are adept at build strong and productive relationships with senior politicians and civil servants; I also know those who struggle to get a meeting and are more often relegated to meetings or 'keeping in touch' calls with more junior civil servants.

So, what should a CEO consider in communicating with senior civil servants and politicians?:

1. **Communication must be engaging and relevant** – either providing information that is of key and urgent importance to the senior civil servant or politicians by clearly informing or aligning with their agenda. A CEO will take time to understand their interests and priorities and ensure that communication reflects how the trust is contributing to this work and furthering it, where appropriate. This is a good basis for instigating and progressing relationships and discussions.

2. **Communication is concise.** The documentation must be short and to the point; time is of the essence. If it is a meeting or a proposal for a meeting, there should be a clear, concise and relevant agenda. Keep briefings to two sides, unless otherwise requested. I have often worked with politicians and senior civil servants whose attention is limited to a few paragraphs, before passing on the information to a more junior official. I've been there!

3. **Try to make communication a habit, but not too much of a habit.** I know one CEO who voluntarily provides their RSC with an update every half term on the work of the trust, its impact, and how it is contributing to area or regional wide priorities for improvement. The briefing is short, to the point, and well presented – reflecting the trust's vision and leadership narrative. Over time the RSC has come to expect this, and when issues arise relating to the trust, the RSC is able to approach them from an informed position and one where relationships are established, open and transparent. A caveat to this, however, communications can be too regular and frequent, giving the sense that the CEO feels either overly accountable to the figure or that they are overly concerned with maintaining their approval. That said, if there are issues or concerns relating to a trust, maintaining regular communication is crucially important and the CEO must keep the RSC updated and always provide 'an open door' where information or discussions can be sought.

Politicians are also important stakeholders. Whilst CEOs should not expect a termly or even annual meeting with the Secretary of State or the minister (there are over one thousand trusts), they should look to communicate with them at least once a year in my view. Adequate investment of time and resource should be spent on this in my view, with CEOs providing a short, relevant and engaging briefing on the trust's progress and priorities once a year, perhaps at the beginning of the year. Even if overlooked, this approach does no harm as the materials also provide the CEO with the basis of a useful introductory document for sharing with other strategic stakeholders when appropriate. The CEO should copy in their local Members of Parliament so that they too can be updated and follow up the communication with the Secretary of State or minister if they feel so inclined. Inviting Members of Parliament on an annual basis to visit the trust and at least one of its schools is also an important way of maintaining a crucial relationship. MPs can help raise awareness of the trust's work and be a helpful advocate when opportunities or issues arise in Westminster or, indeed, in relation to local or regional political issues that impact on its work.

What all of this does is ensure that the trust and CEO take a proactive approach to building those crucial relationships, ensuring that when key developments – positive or negative arise – the politicians and civil servants that have such influence on our organisations are as informed and engaged as possible.

The role of professional capital in CEO development

One final aspect to building external relationships is the fundamental importance they play in a CEO's own professional development. As the most senior person in the organisation, the CEO must look outwards for sources of support, advice and professional learning. As one CEO wrote: 'The thing that was the greatest surprise to me in this job was the intense and profound loneliness.' That can be mitigated. Indeed, two important ways of doing this are through networks and mentors – both of which can provide CEOs with much needed support and solace.

Networks

I am a big proponent of networks, not least having established five regional CEO networks across the UK and having seen the benefits these can have. In a sector as young as the multi-academy trust sector, providing CEOs with access to one another, and with a forum within which they can identify and discuss the key challenges they are all facing in isolation has been enormously helpful. Just because a CEO is in the top job, it doesn't mean they have all the answers! Research tells us that peer-to-peer networks are one of the most effective sources of learning for CEOs. However, it is important that in choosing a CEO network, leaders are discerning about whether they can provide a useful and impactful forum. There are a number of characteristics that are key, all of which I have endeavoured to build into Forum Strategy's own model.

First of all, the network must provide a 'safe haven', where CEOs can express themselves freely and openly in a confidential environment. CEOs will not wish to share all their 'dirty laundry' with their peers, but for the network to work, CEOs need to see it as a place where they can have some of the conversations they are unable to have elsewhere – expressing their worries, concerns, and dilemmas so as to get genuine and useful feedback from their peers. Too many networks in the multi-academy trust world are facilitated by people who also regulate and hold the purse strings to the sector – this is not a good way of encouraging frank and genuinely developmental forums. Ensure that your network provides that 'safe haven'.

Secondly, the network must provide strategic focal points for review and discussion that enables all those involved to participate and gain value. This comes down to the quality of the organisation and facilitation of the network. Does the network identify the common strategic issues that CEOs face and enable them to identify and discuss the key trends and how they apply to their respective organisations? Too many networks are run by people in their spare time, but these networks tend to end up as talking shops around 'what is on our plate', rather than helping leaders to focus in on areas of common challenge and priority.

As we saw earlier in the chapter, all parties must gain something from the partnership for it to sustain. Does the network you belong to sufficiently identify areas of strategic importance that all CEOs can engage with and learn from one another on?

Thirdly, I believe that cross-sector networks are far more valuable than those that are confined to a single industry. The challenges and opportunities faced by those in the CEO role regularly transcend sectors. As we have seen in this book, it is essential that CEOs are 'alive to the world' around them – identifying the trends and changes that face their organisations and how others are responding to them. By moving beyond the structures, terminology, and politics of our own sector, we can reawaken that curiosity that it so essential to developing contextual wisdom. We move beyond the limitations – and limited thinking – of the one sector in order to identify other solutions to the key strategic issues of our times. Whether it be responding to evolving employee expectations, the role of technology and artificial intelligence, or the need to achieve sustainability. Sector-specific networks do have their uses, but they are more useful for those in your senior team rather than for you as CEO.

Does your network invite and involve speakers and contributors from other sectors who have alternative perspectives of key strategic challenges and opportunities? Does the network move your and your peers thinking sufficiently 'out of the box'?

Coaches and mentors

In addition to networks, in my view another essential source of professional development for CEOs is the role of both coaches and mentors.

One of the arguments CEOs sometimes make against coaching is that they should know what to do. After all, aren't they the person who should know all the answers? Then again, one honest CEO quoted in Harvard Business Review put it this way: 'Every night, I go to bed asking myself, 'Why do people think I have all the answers? And every morning I wake up thinking, *is today the day they figure out that I don't?*' This isn't an unusual statement for a CEO to make in private.

The truth is we all need support and guidance to continually improve and find the answers to some of the challenges and stumbling blocks we come across as professional – even at the highest level. An Olympic athlete will have a sports coach and an opera singer at the peak of their career will have a voice coach, so it stands to reason that a CEO should think carefully about whether they would benefit from an executive coach. When asked what the best advice he had ever received was, Eric Schmidt – the former Chairman and CEO of Google – replied: 'to get an executive business coach.' CEO coaching is not a remedial activity, it is about enhancing one's leadership and performance in a role that is enormously challenging and complex. Schmidt also pointed out that at first he was reluctant to receive coaching, and saw the suggestion that he receive it as an inference that his performance wasn't quite where it should be. The truth is that many CEOs have not yet made the leap. Research by Stanford University/The Miles Group of 200 CEOs, board directors, and other senior executives found that two-thirds of CEOs don't receive any outside advice on their leadership skills.

The CEO must be sure that the person they engage as a coach has the credentials to provide the highest standards of coaching. As well as demonstrating credibility – through experience and understanding of what the CEO role entails – experienced CEO coach John Mattone suggests that 'any CEO coach should be prepared to describe their methodology, their assessment tools, and how they plan to measure success. Likewise, they should be strong enough to hold the CEO accountable for doing the work involved in a productive coach-client relationship.' This means much more simply choosing someone who has done the CEO job before and 'knows a thing or two'. As Mattone goes on to say: 'A coach is not a drinking buddy or a shoulder to cry on, but a willing and capable partner in measurable performance improvement.'

A good CEO coach will not teach a CEO how to do the job. That isn't their role. They will, however, help to guide the CEO to become better at reflecting upon and developing their leadership narrative, prioritising the items on their agenda and potentially how they use their time, and considering how they can maximise their personal influence in order to create the legacy they wish to achieve. Self-awareness and a degree of self-regulation should be enhanced through the process.

A coach will keep the process on track, reviewing progress and challenging the CEO to consider both what has gone well (and why), and where headway still needs to be made (and what can be done to ensure it is).

Mentoring, meanwhile, is something that almost every CEO I speak to values, yet how often they access this support varies enormously. How does the mentor role differ from the coach role? Whereas the coaching role is often a paid-for form of training that helps the CEO to work towards a set of clear objectives, the mentoring role is more of a guiding hand – usually provided by an 'experienced elder' who has significant experience from which to draw upon and to share. It is a non-judgmental role; there is no element of accountability or expectation, unlike the coaching role which will include targets and outcomes, driven by the coach.

In choosing a mentor, a CEO should look for the person who can draw on the necessary level of experience, but also the independence, the commitment to confidentiality, and the 'right chemistry' to ensure that the relationship works. A CEO will lay out some of their most pressing challenges and leadership dilemmas to a mentor. Subsequently, they will need to have full confidence in the relationship; where it works, it works well. Harvard Business Review interviewed 45 CEOs who have formal mentoring arrangements and 71% said they were certain that company performance had improved as a result. Strong majorities reported that they were making better decisions (69%) and more capably fulfilling stakeholder expectations (76%). The research went on to conclude that 'more than anything else, these CEOs credited mentors with helping them avoid costly mistakes and become proficient in their roles faster (84%)'.[52]

Within all of this, the onus lies on the CEO to invest the time and energy – and sometimes the resource – in the relationships. It is all too tempting for a CEO to put off coaching and mentoring in the face of a heavy and demanding schedule. The research shows that whilst many CEOs are positive about the idea of coaching and mentoring, putting it into practice is another thing. In the face of such overriding evidence that both coaching and mentoring is highly beneficial to both a CEO's and an organisation's performance, CEOs must speculate to accumulate and invest in both. Sooner, rather than later, if at all possible. An effective CEO will make it a priority to forge these relationships and then commit to them as part of their on-going schedule.

Questions for reflection

- Are you creating a sense of openness and engagement with key local, regional and national stakeholders? Are you prioritising external relationships with reference to strategy and potential impact?

- Are you steering the wider organisation to engage with and embark upon relationships that will add sufficient value to the organisation, whilst avoiding collaborative overload and ensuring there are mutual benefits for all involved?

52. de Janasz, S & Peiperl, M. (2015) 'CEOs Need Mentors Too'. (Harvard Business Review) Available at: https://hbr.org/2015/04/ceos-need-mentors-too

- Are you encouraging the board to play their part in building and maintaining key stakeholder relationships, whilst also ensuring the impact and benefits of all external partnerships are demonstrable and relate sufficiently to core business?

- Are you building open, engaging and constructive relationships with politicians and civil servants, communicating in a way that engages key influencers and ensures that they remain informed about the organisation's work and progress?

- Are you accessing peer to peer networks that are relevant and add value, not least in terms of the CEO and their senior team's professional development?

Chapter 9
Being the CEO

'What we know matters, but who we are matters more.'
– Brene Brown

In writing this book, and through the day-to-day work I do through Forum Strategy, I have had the privilege of meeting CEOs, researching what makes them effective, and observing the growth and development of may successful organisations. I also see first-hand the struggles, the challenges, and the barriers that people taking on this all-pervading yet potentially highly rewarding, role face. I have made the following conclusions, in summary below, about the CEO role.

It requires a careful balance of humility and confidence

The main conclusion I have come to about the job is that success depends upon maintaining a delicate balance of humility and confidence. In my view, both depend on the other. A truly effective CEO has the self-confidence to be humble, to ask the right questions of others; to recognise their areas of weakness in order to identify the support, advisors and expertise they need; and the humility to know that pride almost always comes before a fall! Meanwhile self-confidence is fed by having access to a team of talented people and partners who 'have your back' and bring great expertise and advise to the table; it is generated by the learning process and the wisdom that brings to navigate ever present change; and the confidence to take risks and embrace new opportunities rather than rest on their laurels or wait for the direction of others.

Failing to ensure the balance will almost always see a CEO fail in the end. Too little confidence and employees, boards/shareholders, and partners fail to come along with you. As we have seen, the strength and compelling nature of the leadership narrative matters to every dimension of the role, and the CEO must project belief and commitment to seeing it through, with the support of others.

Yet, more often, successful CEOs become lost in hubris. The self-confidence eclipses the humility, the other essential trait to succeed in role.

In his book, *Mastery*, Robert Greene talks about the notion of emotional pitfalls. He writes of those individuals, like CEOs, who have reached what he describes as the 'Creative-Active' stage of their careers, who are: 'confronted by new challenges that are not simply mental or intellectual. The work is more demanding; we are on our own and the stakes are higher. Our work is now more public and scrutinised. We might have the most brilliant ideas and a mind capable of handling the greatest intellectual challenges, but if we are not careful, we will tumble into emotional pitfalls. We will grow insecure, overly anxious about people's opinions, or excessively self-confident. Or we will become bored and lose a taste for the hard work that is necessary. One we fall into these traps it is hard to extricate ourselves; we lose the necessary perspective to see where we have gone wrong.'

Greene's six emotional pitfalls reflect a battle between humility and confidence

Born out of a lack of confidence

- Conservatism
- Dependency
- Inflexibility

Born out of a lack of humility

- Complacency
- Impatience
- Grandiosity

We all know leaders and CEOs who fell into one of the categories above. In the multi-academy trust sector, we have seen too many leaders who have lacked humility after achieving some big success, demonstrating complacency and impatience in scaling up their organisations without the necessary capacity (people or resources) to maintain their success. They stopped asking the questions they had once asked themselves and assumed that the next level of leadership and organisational development could be achieved by relying on the same ways of doing things.

Some extreme examples have shown grandiosity, in one form or another, embarking on lucrative contracts that they shouldn't have entered into or riding 'rough shod' over their boards in making decisions. These leaders will know only too well to recognise themselves in the words of Greene: 'Once the ego inflates it will only come back to earth through some jarring failure, which will equally scar us.' CEOs must find a way of maintaining perspective.

It is important that CEOs constantly find opportunities to challenge their thinking, to learn from people who are even more successful than they are, and to ensure they are accountable not only to governments and regulators, but to the public they serve.

We also recognise the leaders lacking in confidence. Dependency is a particularly common trait in the academy trust sector. It is often those that attach great significant to government announcements and initiatives, responding and reacting as soon as the Department for Education (DfE) or Ofsted come to a particular position, that suffer from the leadership fatigue this brings. They struggle for the confidence to marry what others expect with the leadership narrative they, their board, and their staff believe in.

Another example is those leaders who are currently chasing pots of money with lengthy lists of criteria attached to the funding, because they lack the confidence to invest in new models of delivery that align with their vision and will deliver sustainable returns for the long term. Inflexibility and conservatism in the face of new challenges such as the financial and recruitment challenges betray a lack of confidence amongst those leaders in making the transition from specialist to CEO. This is a time for radical reforms and new models of employment and delivery, yet it is only those CEOs who can generate confidence through having the right teams of people and access to the right advice who will thrive.

For those who have found the balance, this is an exciting time to be a CEO. They sense the challenge and the risk of taking on this job and the need to bring others along with them – there lies the humility. They also sense the opportunities to be seized for their end users, be they pupils, clients, patients, or otherwise; and they recognise within themselves the ability to make things happen – to be the conductors of the orchestra.

In meeting with many dozens of CEOs I have come to recognise this: a great CEO will tell you how much they love their job and how humbled they are to do it.

Alignment and investment: The relationship with the board

This is the cement between the four foundations of the role. I have written at length about it in Chapter 4. If the CEO and the board are not aligned on mission, vision and values, then there is no point in continuing.

The prospective CEO must 'weigh up' their board as much as the board weighs up them! A lack of alignment leads to a very unhappy situation for a good CEO, so choose your board carefully. Once in role, a CEO should have no control over who sits on the board – and that is why so much time needs to be invested in making the relationship work. Most of the time, with that investment, it will.

A CEO who seeks the challenge and advice of their board, who contributes to their thinking by offering their professional perspective and facilitating the inputs of other experts, and who communicates with them well and avoids landing them with surprises, will create the basis for a successful relationship.

Connecting, connecting, connecting! Then communication, communication, communication!

The leadership narrative defines everything – the culture, the strategy, the relationships, and what is prioritised within the organisation.

Ownership of the narrative matters, and that is why the CEO seeks to translate the board's vision into a narrative that relates to everyone within the organisation and is tangible and compelling enough to define the day to day work of the organisations.

The CEO will reflect their clients/end users', employees', and partners' stories back to them – acting as the chief storyteller in the process and exemplifying what values and success look like in action. That requires a lot of listening and learning, but it ensures the narrative is relevant and inspiring. The CEO doesn't need to be a charismatic figure, but they do need to shape that narrative and then communicate it.

A CEO's work in communicating the narrative never ends. Clients/end users, staff and partners need to hear the story and be reminded of the organisation's purpose and direction on a regular basis. The connection must be made as new relationships are formed and solidified. This is the basis of organisational behaviour and of attracting the right people and partners to work for and with the organisation.

Building a team of experts

The transition from specialist leader to CEO is defined by the team dynamic. You are no longer the expert in the room, you are the person accountable for everything that happens within the organisation – be that the core work (which may historically be your area of specialism), HR, finance, IT, data protection, health and safety, recruitment, sites and premises, insurance, and so on.

No effective CEO is an island. They are the leader and facilitator of a team of experts who they serve by providing direction, support, challenge and – yes – the ultimate decisions. CEOs, again, are humble about the fact they neither have the capacity or the range of expertise to deliver the organisation's remit; yet they have the self-confidence to set direction and make decisions through the fact they understand this and build the necessary team of experts around them.

It therefore goes without saying that a CEO cannot succeed without their team. A good CEO sees recruiting to that team and maintaining a positive culture across that team as central to what they do. They are also uncompromising when a member fails to live the values or continuously underperforms. The success of a CEO is defined by the quality of their team.

Leading with values and ethics

The good CEO recognises that everyone else in the organisation watches everything they do. Their words, their actions, their deeds are scrutinised more than ever in the world of social media and 24-hour news. Congruency is at the heart of the CEO role. People need and expect us to stay true. Where we don't, failure – sooner or later – is inevitable.

Realising you are an 'enabler' not a 'driver'

Capacity, culture, 'good' data, processes and innovation matter.

This – together with building your team – is the essence of the step up to the role of the CEO. There is a certain amount of letting go in the transition, entailing a change in leadership mindset whereby the CEO knows they cannot control or direct activity at every level of the organisation. They simply cannot be the manager, coach or guide to everyone as they may have been previously in a specialist leadership role.

This is about creating the conditions for good delivery and improvement and innovation. Again, it begins with a compelling leadership narrative, but the CEO must take the lead in 'enabling' the organisation with the necessary capacity and expertise, the on-going monitoring and intelligence (data), the necessary systems and processes, and the research and development culture that give rise to improvement and innovation at scale. Once in place, the CEO's role is to ask the right questions and to review the process.

Are you an investor CEO or a bean counter CEO?

In times of austerity, and at a time when the pace of change is unprecedented, CEOs cannot afford to be overly conservative. Money must be spent wisely and efficiently, but that can't be at the expense of improvement and innovation – including designing and delivering new models of service delivery that reduce costs in the long run. Investment entails some element of risk, and the effective CEO will balance that risk with a need to respond to the challenges facing their organisation. The bean counter CEO is limited not only in what they can achieve, but ultimately, the costs they can shave from the same old methods of delivery. This is a time for CEOs who see their budgets as the beginning, rather than the limit of what is possible.

Remember, you are not island

You are not an island – individually or organisationally; the world is too complex and fast-paced for splendid isolation.

Complexity, austerity, and the pace of change, have all been key contextual themes within this book. None is likely to go away any time soon. In a world of greater independency and where organisational resources are stretched, the strategic partnerships forged by the CEO become crucial. A good CEO will constantly be asking the question: which organisations, groups and people do we need to be working with in a mutually beneficial and sustainable way? Prioritising the most essential relationships will mean that a CEO can avoid collaborative overload, but they must also work hard to forge such partnerships with a commitment to mutual-respect, generosity, and positive outcomes for all involved.

Finally

Finally, an effective CEO will embrace the opportunities for coaching and mentoring and the power of well-run peer-to-peer networking. They will recognise that the role is complex, often unpredictable and – to a degree – lonely, and that high quality support and counsel from trusted sources is essential to thriving in the role. In the words of the writer, Margaret Wheatley: 'The primary way to prepare for the unknown is to attend to the quality of our relationships today'.[53] The quality of the relationships we forge is, most probably, the most crucial factor in our quest for success in being the CEO.

---

53. Wheatley, M. (2007) *Finding Our Way: Leadership for an Uncertain Time.* San Francisco, California: Berrett-Koehler Publishers.

Appendices

Appendix 1: Six things that set the CEO role apart from executive headteachers

What is clear is that the CEO role is still very new to the education sector and there is certainly no single, defining approach to the job. What's encouraging is that an air of mystery surrounds the role in other sectors too – with a CEO's success depending on context, resources, timing, and luck as well as leadership. This is why so many CEOs are natural risk takers and can live with a fair degree of ambiguity and uncertainty. It comes with the territory. As I say in the book, there's no OS map for navigating the CEO role, just guiding constellation of stars in the night sky, at best. The CEO can, with a clear sky, put themselves at an advantage by reflecting on the role, and considering how they use the influence inherent within it to raise the chances of success.

A key issue for new and aspirant MAT CEOs is 'making the leap' from executive headteacher (or sometimes, even, from headteacher) to the CEO role. So, what are the key differences between the two, based on what I've learned from my research and my interactions with over a hundred CEOs both within and beyond the MAT sector? Here are six:

1. You are the accounting officer
The buck really does stop with you, not with the local authority or someone else further up the tree that you can refer the issue to. That

brings an added weight of responsibility and accountability, which means ethics and values are at a premium. The job can feel very lonely, but it shouldn't do. Whilst some CEOs fall under the weight, others embrace a new level of autonomy and freedom that, if supported by the right team of people around them and a high calibre board, can manifest itself in greater innovation and a greater ability to respond to the needs of those you serve. The good CEO maintains a 'direct line of sight' to the frontline – be it the pupils in the classroom, the hospital ward, or the shop floor.

2. You will find yourself leading diverse teams of professionals who are 'the experts'

This is a defining shift. The headteacher or executive headteacher generally leads a senior leadership team of those who belong to the same profession. You are still seen as the 'expert in the room'. A CEO does not generally work within the same SLT dynamic. As I say in the book, this is the move from 'expert in chief' to 'learner in chief'. The mindset must change from being 'the person to ask' to the person who knows enough about each discipline and how to view specialist issues through a strategic, whole organisation lens. A good CEO will listen, listen hard, review all the facts and advice, and take the decision, often on the best advice of their people and through a good dose of intuition fed by their years of learning and experience. That is inherently risky, and so the good CEO spends so much of their time building a team of talents who are far better than them.

3. You will enable rather than drive improvement

This is a major transition for anyone who continues to be a CEO in an organisation where the 'bread and butter' work is also the CEO's area of professional expertise. An executive head drives improvement. These roles – such as National Leaders of Education and Local Leaders – are about leading from the front, demonstrating what success looks like on a day to day basis, and coaching colleagues on specialist functions. The CEO cannot do this – it is unsustainable. There are simply not enough hours in the week, nor should an organisation become so reliant on one person's specialist knowledge. Instead, the CEO creates the conditions through which improvement becomes an organisational habit; setting the vision for what improvement looks like and creating the capacity, culture, processes, accountabilities, and investment in innovation and research, that ensures improvement becomes the 'lifeblood' of the organisation. Some experienced NLEs and LLEs make this transition, others cling on for dear life to the job of school improvement leader – fearing they are doing themselves out of a job. A good CEO is always doing themselves out of a job! (See our seven pillars of improvement at scale here)

4. You must prioritise the sustainable development of the organisation

This means taking responsibility for the 'whole organisation' and the inter-dependencies between school improvement, HR, finance, technology, health and safety, governance and otherwise. The executive head can get away with employing a business manager who may be an accountant and can ensure budgets are balanced and some economies of scale are achieved. I am firmly of the view that a good CEO needs an experienced chief operating officer, who can ensure operational delivery across the board, ensuring that the organisation is investing strategically in its people, its resources, and its relationships with others externally, to ensure the quality of provision the CEO expects. In an age defined by austerity and complexity, the CEO needs someone with an entrepreneurial mindset at their side, because maximising income and resources for this generation of children and their educational experience is at a premium.

Entrepreneurial leadership is not a 'dirty phrase' anymore; it is a moral imperative. Simply cutting where we can and hoping for politicians to be generous is to fail in the defining challenge for this generation of leaders. To succeed here, a CEO requires someone who has experience of the world of enterprise, customer service, and organisational development, not simply restricted to that of budgets and procurement. This probably will – at this moment in time, at least – require the CEO to look beyond, rather than within, the sector for talent.

5. You will have an even wider outlook on the world.

As accounting officer and having the autonomy and freedoms they have, a CEO will need to foster a broader set of relationships internally

179

and externally. Internally, given the size of the organisations they lead, they will need to 'step up' the way in which they communicate, sharing their leadership narrative through a range of mediums and events, and repeating it often, with authenticity and clarity. This will also help them to clarify their message externally, which will become even more essential. The organisation is not an island, it will – particularly in an age of austerity and complexity – need to engage and involve a wide range of stakeholders. The CEO must lead on this, being discerning in which partnerships align with organisational strategy (and which will just sap time and energy) and taking time to develop positive and constructive relationships with a broad list of stakeholders who they maintain relationships with – not least ministers and local politicians, local businesses, health leaders, and community groups to name a few. This is the age of leadership for generating social and professional capital, and the CEO is at the heart of that.

6. Your professional development and support is even more important (not less so) now you are CEO.

CEOs need to invest time in understanding the politics and the political dynamics their organisations are operating within – this is not simply about responding to education policy, it is about playing your part in education policy development and sector 'thought-leadership' wherever possible. This is your professional development. It's also about having a broader view to changes in charity law, employment law, health and safety regulations and economic regeneration projects – all of which may impact your organisation. Social and economic issues must be monitored and anticipated, feeding into strategic planning. Currently these can include, for example, risks and opportunities of emerging technologies, the changing nature of the jobs market and employee expectations, and understanding trends such as worsening mental health issues and how to mitigate these.

The CEO should embrace the advice and guidance of a board of trustees who can bring a level of insight appropriate to the scale of the organisation and its influence. Not having access to a good board is a real danger for a CEO and should be a big consideration when taking on the job. The role also requires the CEO to set aside the necessary time for strategic reflection and planning. This is something our weekly

#MATLeaders briefings help to facilitate, given that some CEOs struggle to set even an hour aside to this in any given week. Finally, the transition to CEO also usually involves a transition in executive support. You need executive support of the highest standard – a PA or executive assistant who can interact confidently and on your behalf with senior external stakeholders and governing board members, and who can fulfil the role of managing the CEO's diary – something that has a direct link to your ability to do the job, and to do it well.

Appendix 2: Creating a culture of 'collective commitment' across a multi-academy trust

Originally published at www.forumstrategy.org, 2017.

A key premise of successful multi-academy trusts is their ability to draw upon and mobilise the skills and talents of staff across their schools to achieve improvements in more schools and for more children. Indeed, sustainable and successful school improvement models depend not only on sufficient professional expertise and sound and scalable improvement processes, but also on the capacity of a wide-range of professionals to provide coaching, mentoring, CPD, peer review, and – at times – substantive leadership or teaching support.

Yet, challenges and barriers to collective school improvement can easily present themselves. Achieving cultural commitment to whole-trust success, in a context where leaders are highly accountable for individual schools, can be challenging. Leaders are also – quite rightly – invested emotionally and professionally in 'their schools'. Finding a balance, however, is key to the collective success of all schools and all children in academy trusts. Here, we look at how Focus Academy Trust (Focus-Trust) developed a cultural commitment to 'collective efficacy' across their trust and what they plan to do next.

Starting point

'We began from a position of values,' says Helen Rowland, CEO of (Focus-Trust). 'Our values are Fair, Care, Share, Dare and have always underpinned our commitment: Learning Together, Making a Difference. That applies to our trust and to our fifteen academies. We're in it for all children and we work together to make a difference for all our children. That's the starting point.'

Indeed, the values were very much key to the successful early development of the trust, ensuring that its journey to a place where it had nine schools by the start of 2015 was based on collective commitment and making the best use of staff across schools. However, Helen was also conscious that when the trust expanded beyond nine schools it would be difficult to maintain the depth of relationships and proximity that had underpinned the trust's journey to that point: 'We knew from existing evidence that trusts moving to more than five or six schools really need to invest in reinforcing, and systemizing to a degree, the culture and the behaviours that generate school improvement at scale. We were very much drawn to the concept of 'teacher collective efficacy' based on John Hattie's research and the evidential basis it provides for success for all pupils in individual schools. We saw through our work around visible learning what a profound and important role collective efficacy has in individual schools. There is a firm recognition now that all teachers and staff have an important role to play in – and accountability for – securing the best outcomes for children. We wanted to make that a reality at a trust level as we grew further. Just as schools can get even better through collective commitment to all pupils, so too do trusts through collective commitment to improving outcomes in all academies.

'Trusts moving to more than five or six schools really need to invest in reinforcing, and systemizing to a degree, the culture and the behaviours that generate school improvement at scale.'

Changing mindsets

The trust's strategy was to begin with a trust-wide conversation with principals to revisit the importance of collective commitment to the school improvement model and the role that they needed to play in that. Helen was particularly keen to revisit the values and commitment – the onus on learning and making a difference together, and the importance of leaders in the trust seeing themselves, first and foremost, as contributors to trust-wide success rather than as a receiver of support or provision from the trust.

Indeed, the need for change was partly driven by what Helen describes as a culture of care and concern rather than shared responsibility and ownership. Heads and senior leaders cared about other schools in the trust and were encouraging of their colleagues' progress, but there was – to a degree – a lack of positive action or sense of accountability for improvement in other schools. 'We are only as strong as our weakest academy,' says Helen, 'and it was important that we all accepted a sense of moral accountability and responsibility to each academy's success. We didn't want a centre-led model whereby principals and schools saw it as being a handful of people's responsibility to improve our weakest academies; that absolutely isn't the premise that sustainable and successful MATs are based on. Each time an academy joined our trust I wanted the school improvement to strengthen, and for leaders – in whatever circumstances they were in – to recognise their responsibility to contribute to the success of all academies and children and young people. It was about changing the language so that it was about 'our academies' rather than 'my academy' or 'their academies'.'

The discussions led to greater sense of ownership amongst principals. 'The philosophy has gradually changed,' says Helen. 'We began to see leaders deepen their commitment and their enthusiasm for supporting other academies. Principals were more ready and willing to release their deputies and assistant heads for secondments in other schools, which is a big ask at times, because it was increasingly recognised as being part of our trust's moral imperative.' Indeed, such generosity has played a crucial role in the recent improvement of a number of schools in challenging circumstances and has also seen senior and middle leaders develop their leadership skills. Principals are also using the secondment of their staff as an opportunity to promote high potential middle leaders for periods of time to gain experience and development.

Tangible strategies
However, Helen and her team have also been mindful that cultural commitment must be reinforced and supported by tangible strategies and processes. The trust – as part of its annual residential conference – encouraged all staff to develop pledges around how they will contribute to the wider success of the trust. These pledges are wide-ranging and dependent on the individual's role and the level at which they operate, but only serve to reinforce the trust-wide commitment. The trust has also introduced a certificate scheme that recognises individual schools for their contribution to trust-wide success. Examples include where a school has given up time or resource in support of another school's improvement or where a school has made a significant contribution to trust-wide CPD. The Trust Board has also contributed to this shift in culture, establishing the role of Principal Advisory Representatives who provide the board with a 'trust-wide' academies perspective on school

improvement issues. Trustees are now advocates for each academy. Each Trustee visits and attends meetings in the academy and champions their successes/needs.

In addition, the trust has also established a range of professional networks for different roles, with the expectation that all schools attend to share best practice, to access learning from other academies, and to hear key trust-wide information, national updates and the latest research. In this vein, all year group teachers from Reception to Year 6 meet regularly to share practice in books, resources, planning striving and engage in moderation activity to improve the outcomes of all children across the trust.

'The ethos of peer review has done a great deal to create a strong sense of shared responsibility for improvement amongst our principals and staff.'

Central to the development of collective efficacy across Focus has been the fact that heads and the trust itself have modelled collaboration for shared improvement. The trust has made the development of peer review between schools (in partnership with the Education Development Trust) a key priority in its efforts to create relationships between schools that are based on trust, honesty, mutual-respect and a commitment to collective improvement. Through peer review, triads of principals and improvement champions undertake reviews of one another's schools, providing constructive feedback on practice and any follow-up support they can. 'The ethos of peer review has done a great deal to create a strong sense of shared responsibility for improvement amongst our principals and staff,' says Helen. 'That is because we are all participants in a process that is focused on moving schools along – not judging them. When principals and improvement champions take part in the reviews of another school – which is focused on constructive and considerate feedback based on professional expertise – they genuinely want to bring something to the table and to help that other school to learn and take forward its areas for development.'

In addition to the expectation that principals are involved in review, a recently new component of a Focus-Trust principal's role is to provide coaching support to another colleague, and Heads of Academy are also providing coaching to deputies in other schools within the trust to support their leadership development. There has always been an expectation in the trust that all schools will share their data with others to inform improvement, identify areas in need of support, and encourage the sharing of practice between schools.

At a trust level, Focus is also modelling collective efficacy. Key members of the SLT and trust board have been involved in MAT to MAT peer review through Forum Education's programme, supporting another medium-sized MAT to reflect on how it can develop an even stronger culture of collective efficacy amongst its headteachers and wider teams. The trust has also shared key staff with other local MATs when their schools have faced particular challenges, including one example where a Principal was seconded to another local trust for a couple of terms.

Next steps

The trust is now determined to further embed the renewed sense of collective efficacy that has developed over the last two years. The trust held another conference earlier this month to bring principals together to consider trust-wide needs and priorities, and to reflect on how collective efficacy is taking hold and how it can be evidenced. 'We have agreed, as a group of professionals, that this is about 'a shared commitment to working together on the things that matter to improve outcomes for all pupils,' says Helen. 'The next step is how we all further work towards making that a reality.'

The next steps certainly seek to build in more accountability. Principals now feel ready and positive about committing personally to the notion of trust-wide accountability, and this will be embedded through the appraisal process that provides all principals with a trust-wide responsibility and a corresponding performance measure. These appraisal objectives have been carefully discussed with the principals based on trust priorities, what they can contribute and what is realistically achievable within the year ahead. Helen believes this is already having tangible impact in terms of school-to-school improvement.

There are also plans to ensure that a commitment to collective improvement and success is prioritised within the recruitment process and that all candidates are expected to demonstrate an understanding of and a commitment to the success of the wider-trust, reflective of the level and nature of their responsibilities. 'I was really encouraged,' says Helen, 'by a recent recruitment round where the successful candidate spoke to a number of our Principals, learning about them and how they reflected the trust's values. That person wanted to know that there was a strong sense of collective commitment and what collaboration looked like in practice. I think we should be expecting that same level of interest and commitment to other academies in our future appointments – especially to the most senior leadership roles.'

Finally, as with many other aspects of successful trust development, there is a dependency on geographical proximity either between all schools in the trust, or geographical hubs, to make this work. School improvement, and the role of staff at all levels in contributing to it, becomes more challenging the further afield schools are, and Helen and her team at Focus-Trust are determined to retain the geographical proximity between schools wherever possible and develop clusters where that may be a challenge.

Key learning points:

- It is important to establish and reinforce the commitment to collective efficacy through regular dialogue between leaders and staff generally. This conversation must be very much grounded in the values and vision of the trust.

- MAT leaders should communicate the evidential grounding for school-to-school improvement, including the development opportunities leaders can gain through supporting other schools and the opportunity to develop and retain high potential staff with 'stretch opportunities'. The NLE model showed the 'mutual improvement' benefits of schools supporting other schools.

- Language is important. It is crucial that key trust documents, processes, meeting papers and agendas, and the dialogue in leadership meetings reflect the collective commitment to and ownership of all schools improvement. Senior leaders should carefully model the language of 'collective efficacy', including the use of 'our schools'.

- Celebrate contributions to collective improvement and success, whether through case studies and articles, or through certificate schemes or at trust-wide events.

- Embed a sense of trust wide responsibility and accountability within principals' job descriptions and appraisal documentation where possible.

- A culture of peer review between schools, with heads and SLT members at the centre, can help to embed a sense of shared responsibility for improvements in other schools. Is participation in school-to-school peer review part of your heads' role?

- Place an onus on commitment to trust-wide improvement and the success of other schools within the recruitment process for senior leadership positions.

- Remember that geographical proximity has an important bearing on people's ability and willingness to contribute to the improvement of other schools.

- Trust-wide professional networks with a focus on improvement and professional development are key to developing a sense of collective support and commitment to other schools; ensure all schools, all of the time, attend these.

Appendix 3: Cementing a strong and scalable school improvement model at Flying High

Originally published at www.forumstrategy.org, 2017.

Origins of the school improvement model

The Flying High Trust is a primary-only trust of 16 schools working across Nottinghamshire and Derbyshire. As with many multi-academy trusts, the origins of Flying High can be found in the National Leaders of Educations' (NLE) initiative, which was launched by the National College in 2007. Chris Wheatley, the CEO of Flying High was – like many of today's academy trust chief executives – one of those designated as an NLE to provide intensive leadership support for schools in challenging circumstances. The initiative was unique at the time in that, rather than taking successful heads out of their schools and parachuting them into schools needing support, it encouraged successful leaders to remain in position at their original school, whilst providing consultancy style support to other schools for an agreed period of time. The NLE model was very much focused on school improvement without putting the quality of other schools at risk. Indeed, evidence showed that NLEs' own schools generally tended to achieve continued improvements despite the NLE's work elsewhere.

'We were very motivated by the NLE model because it was so focused on school improvement without compromise. In fact it was mutually beneficial because we refined and improved our own practice further through providing support to others,' says Chris. 'We entered into some really positive partnerships and we achieved some very positive improvements in those struggling schools. The NLE work really showed us how collaboration could achieve school improvement, but there was no framework or structure for a sustained relationship in most cases. Whilst some of the schools that were supported went on to do well, others struggled with the lack of direction and continued support from an NLE. It was rewarding and frustrating in equal measure!'

As with many leaders, Chris saw the opportunity to create a more sustained school improvement model through the development of a multi-academy trust. 'My vision was based on achieving self-sustaining school improvement, which was informed by much of thinking at that time – such as David Hargreaves' thinkpieces and the Sinagpore model. We wanted to move things on and create sustained improvement relationships between schools and practitioners, rather than waving goodbye at the end of a deployment and not having any further responsibility for what happened in those schools. Our vision also included the notion of shared accountability, openness between schools, the ability to deploy talent freely across schools when and where it was needed, and also the freedom to share resources. The NLE model had broken down barriers and encouraged a culture of school to school support. However, we wanted to create a school improvement model for the long term.'

The golden rule and building capacity

Chris established the Flying High Trust in 2012. The trust's initial growth saw four schools join in quick succession – three that were rated by Ofsted as 'Outstanding' or 'Good' and one that needed support. Much of this growth owed itself to the relationships developed through the NLE work and the Candleby Lane Teaching School Alliance, which was established in 2011. 'There was an enthusiasm for even deeper partnership,' says Chris, 'but it was built on a commitment to the long-term success of all our schools and children, and that required a culture of deeper partnership – one that was honest, challenging, open and based on a shared determination for success in every school. The MAT model, we felt, would involve a much deeper commitment to schools that were struggling and would also help us to keep improving our successful schools and help them to avoid complacency.'

Chris' vision required a strong school improvement model. However, that first had to be underpinned by bringing on board the necessary capacity. The trust was mindful of those trusts that – in their enthusiasm or otherwise – had expanded too quickly and had put great strain on resources and the capacity of their teachers and leaders, leading to failure. 'We quickly came to devise a golden rule that we would have three Good or Outstanding schools for every RI or special measures school in the trust. The model we wanted to create would rely heavily on our internal capacity for improvement – so this ratio became the non-negotiable from an early stage or else it would not work.'

The need for time and resource for school improvement was not underestimated. This was in part because Chris and his team believed that intensive support – the 'tightening up' approach as he describes it – was required for those schools in challenging circumstances. Indeed, in the early days of the trust's development, as with many CEOs, Chris was extremely hands on in providing monitoring and evaluation, coaching and support, and modelling leadership within the trust's requires improvement school. The school improvement model at that stage – although able to draw on expertise and resource from elsewhere in the trust – was not unlike the NLE model in that it fundamentally relied on Chris, only it came with even more accountability and responsibility! The school improvement model could have remained in his head, but he was clear that as the trust grew further, he needed to step back and build the capacity and systems for wide-scale quality assurance and improvement.

From Executive Head to CEO: Letting go of day-to-day school improvement

For many trust CEOs this is the most personally challenging experience of trust growth. Recent DfE advice warned growing MATs of the danger of too much over-reliance on the skills, expertise and knowledge of an executive leader who is seeing their wider leadership role grow, yet often seeing their school improvement responsibilities expand too. Yet, for many leaders, letting go of the reigns of day-to-day school improvement is hard when they have grown to see it as their 'bread and butter'. Many executive leaders owe their careers up to that stage on their ability in turning schools around. However, this stepping back is a necessary exercise for CEOs within growing trusts, and appointing the right people to step into the work they are leaving behind is probably the most critical moment in growth.

For Flying High, the first key appointment in this area was Graeme Robins, Director of School Improvement and Quality Assurance. The role was created by Chris and the Chair of Trustees for someone with significant experience of providing leadership and achieving school improvement across a number of schools, and as a Local Leader of Education and former Executive Headteacher, Graeme fitted the bill well. Graeme's role initially involved interim executive leadership to one school, whilst also providing quality assurance and facilitating school improvement across the initial group of four. The appointment immediately allowed Chris to step back as the demands of running a growing trust increased– including line and performance managing a wide range of staff. 'Appointing someone with Grahams' calibre and experience into that post was essential to the successful development of the trust,' says Chris, 'I could immediately trust him to draw on years of experience in school improvement and quality assurance and to be confident in acting with sufficient autonomy.'

As the trust grew, Chris recruited two more Quality Assurance (QA) leads to work alongside Graeme. Chris and Graeme were of the view that, given the level of insight and knowledge required of each school, the role would become unsustainable beyond a cluster of eight schools. Where the QA lead was also an executive head, the cluster they are responsible is limited to six schools.

Distributing school improvement responsibility

It also became clear that the role of quality assurance and school improvement had to be split. Providing both could sometimes be conflicting and – as the clusters grew – it was also became extremely time consuming for directors to do it alone. As a result– whilst maintaining key responsibility for monitoring and checking standards across the schools – it was decided that the three directors of QA would delegate key school improvement aspects of their work to a group of serving heads within the trust – known internally as Heads + 1. This has involved identifying heads (through a rigorous performance management process) with the necessary capacity and experience to provide support to their peers and to other schools.

As a result, these heads – alongside their day-to-day roles – are now playing a leading role in providing school improvement across the trust. They are taking on responsibility in a number of ways, including through coaching their peers, providing training and joint practice development for leaders and teachers, and supporting the development of the curriculum and assessment systems in other schools. The quality assurance directors are line and performance managed by Chris as CEO, and those heads with a school improvement role are performance managed by Chris too (although QA directors are responsible for their day-to-day line management).

Embedding the systems and processes

Alongside the appointment of the additional directors of quality assurance and the wider distribution of school improvement leadership, the trust has also worked hard to embed its systems and processes for school improvement and quality assurance. 'The improvement model is not reactive,' says Chris, 'The systems and processes allow us to regularly monitor changes in data, the quality of teaching and children's work, and the concerns of heads so that we can identify issues and respond quickly by deploying the most appropriate kind of support. That is where the QA role really feeds into and determines the nature of school improvement – and for schools that are struggling the QA needs to be very active because the support needs of these schools are evolving all the time.'

Each school within the trust receives a quality assurance visit from the directors of QA – the frequency of which is determined by the school's individual circumstances. For those that are in challenging circumstances, these can take place every four weeks (and some schools in these circumstances may also be receiving day-to-day leadership from one of the QA directors as a part-time executive head), whilst for those that are performing well, these take place – on average – every six weeks.

The visits include reviewing data (including pupil progress and outcomes; attendance; and exclusions), conversations with the head and senior team, lesson observations, observations of the learning environment, pupil-voice discussions, and book scrutinies.

Information management: oversight and school improvement planning

The quality assurance visits ensure that key information is captured and that it informs the trust's two key school improvements documents – the school's quality assurance visit pro formas and the school's Individual School Action Plan (ISAP), both of which are reviewed at the trust SLT's six-weekly risk review meetings.

The schools' quality assurance visit pro formas are more summative in nature, and provide a snapshot of the school's performance based on the data and the outcomes of QA visits. The dashboards include information on pupil outcomes, progress, attendance, behaviour, and general concerns/issues raised by the heads. These are reviewed at the SLT's six-weekly review meetings and by the cluster's local governing bodies and provide both a useful accountability tool and a means of comparing performance across the cluster. They are also key to determining the level and nature of support agreed within the ISAP.

The ISAPs set out the level and nature of school improvement that each school requires (informed by the quality assurance visit), and provides a clear overview of who is involved and responsible for achieving improvement and by when. The action plans evolve in response to the information gathered through the visits, and are the key documents in ensuring that everyone involved is clear about a school's improvement priorities and plans. The school's headteacher, director of QA, and the director of the teaching school alliance are all involved in writing and agreeing the ISAP (together with setting key targets and agreeing costings of school improvement).

It is through these visits and documents, and also through their performance management of heads, that the directors of QA are able to determine the next steps to enable all schools to be able to move to the next level. Those next steps can involve bespoke school improvement and CPD provided by Heads + 1, the teaching school, and other trust experts such as NLEs and Lead Practitioners. The documents are also used by the Flying High Trust's Pupil, School and Strategic Party to analyse each school's progress and to hold leaders (including directors of QA and the CEO) to account. Headline information on the progress of each cluster and key schools is also shared at the termly meetings of the trust's directors.

Flying High's ethos for school improvement

In line with Chris' initial vision, the school improvement model at Flying High is about ensuring accountability, but the emphasis is heavily weighted on making sure that each school has a plan that is well-informed, bespoke, and underpinned by key actions and targets for improvement that are only made possible through a strong culture of school-to-school support. The model is also very much focused on providing individual schools with ownership of their improvement, with heads and SLTs involved in identifying the QA data and in identifying 'next steps' with their directors of QA through the ISAPs. The regular and routine nature of the process (including regular review and oversight), as well as the ease of access to wide ranging trust-wide support, is key to the model's success. Indeed, five of the trusts schools have now received an Ofsted inspection since joining Flying High, with each school seeing an improvement in its inspection grading.

Chris is very aware that as the trust grows, his own role in performance managing those heads with school improvement responsibility may need to change, and the trust is looking at how – through the deputy CEO and the executive team – it can ensure that there remains sufficient executive oversight of school improvement as the trust grows. It is likely that Chris will continue to line manage the directors of quality assurance through the next stage of growth.

Key documents and meetings

Quality assurance visits vary in frequency and duration depending on the school's position. These can take place once every four to six weeks and involve data analysis, learning walks, pupil voice discussion, meetings with the head and senior leaders, and lesson observations.

Quality assurance visit dashboards provides a wide ranging overview of key data for each school. These are updated after each QA visit and reviewed by LGBs across the school's cluster. These dashboards inform the ISAP and are a key document for enabling leaders to hold schools to account for progress and performance over time.

Individual School Action Plans are updated after each QA visit, these set out the school's improvement priorities and plans for school to school improvement. The ISAP will signpost to specific support, including the nature of support required, the cost and the desired outcomes.

Risk review meetings take place every six weeks and attended by QA directors and CEO. Review each school's ongoing progress against improvement plans, with reference to the school improvement plan, and quality assurance visit dashboards.

Local Governing Body (LGB) cluster meetings provide an opportunity for LGBs to scrutinise data across schools;

Trust board meetings. Trustees review high level data from across clusters;

Key learning points for growing MATs:

- Is there an over reliance on the executive leader? Is this at the expense of systemised processes, knowledge capture and bringing in additional expertise to drive school-improvement at scale?

- Is there sufficient capacity within the trust to drive school improvement whilst also ensuring the standards in its well performing schools are maintained? Flying High work to a 3:1 ratio of good and outstanding schools to requires improvement/ special measures schools.

- Appointments to executive Quality Assurance and School Improvement roles are crucial. Ensure you employ someone with expertise and experience of undertaking this work successfully elsewhere, particularly in the early stages of your trust's growth. Do not, for example, be tempted to promote up someone who is a good head but without experience of driving improvement across schools – it's unlikely that you will have the capacity to train and support them!

- Is there sufficient separation of school improvement and quality assurance roles? The Flying High Trust have created a model where the quality assurer has a role in line managing and deploying school improvement leads, but performance management of SI leads is undertaken alongside the CEO.

- Is school improvement responsibility sufficiently distributed in order to maximise the skills and expertise of individuals across the trust?

- Is reporting regular and routine enough so that evolving needs and challenges can be identified and responded to as quickly as possible?

Appendix 4: An Executive Summary of Forum Strategy's 3rd #MATLeaders Policy Roundtable Report: Sustainability through an age of austerity

Originally published at www.forumstrategy.org, December 2018.

Forum Strategy's third policy roundtable event took place on 15th November 2018. This event was held in response to on-going concerns regarding funding for the school and wider education sector. There was a desire to think more creatively about how leaders – across the MAT sector in particular – could work to ensure that not only efficiencies can be made but also income can be generated, and more funding retained within the sector, and services for pupils further improved.

In order to gain the views and perspectives of MAT leaders in this important area, Forum Strategy posed the following key questions to those MAT CEOs, trustees and others attending the roundtable event:

- How are trusts maximising their resources and expertise to improve pupils' education experiences, whilst achieving better value for money?

- What kind of skills, expertise and experience is necessary to maximise resources within and across trusts, whilst generating additional income and social capital to benefit pupils?

- How can government (aside from increasing funding) better support trusts to achieve innovation and create sustainable services for themselves and the wider system? What are the risks and how can governance and ethical leadership ensure a values-led approach to new organisational models?

The discussion at the roundtable event has informed the following key points which it was felt should be considered by colleagues across the MAT sector, as well as the Department for Education, in order to inform their consideration of and planning for sustainability during an era of on-going austerity.

Maximising resources and expertise

1. There is great scope for individual MATs and the wider sector to realise greater efficiencies and to generate income from a wide

range of provision (keeping more funding within the sector). However, this must be driven by the needs of children and young people at its heart, and must not be ethically at odds with this moral purpose.

2. When considering the potential to develop and provide/sell a service, MATs (or groups of MATs) need to ensure they first test the market to determine whether there is a genuine need for what they are planning to offer, and whether this is likely to be sustainable over the longer term.

3. MATs should not be afraid to offer traded services, provided that any surplus funds are ploughed back into the MAT and its schools. Indeed, trading in order to generate additional revenue and ensure the on-going viability of important services is common in the charity sector. MATs are often able to provide key services at a reduced cost to other MATs and schools, and to a high standard. MATs and their boards must carefully consider the legal implications of trading and adhere to these. The 'cost' of ensuring this – assuming it is reasonable – should be considered as an investment in long-term sustainability.

4. MAT leaders and boards should consider whether their trust leadership teams have become too 'top-heavy' – perhaps in preparation for anticipated growth that has not yet been realised – and how staffing arrangements at the centre could be made more efficient and sustainable. MATs should also consider whether they have the right people 'on the bus' given the growth they are experiencing/have experienced and the demand for more sustainable and innovative delivery models. It was considered that, whilst recognising that senior financial expertise is essential, many CEOs would benefit from the wider remit and operational delivery experience of a Chief Operating Officer in addition to, or instead of, a Chief Finance Officer. The CFO role could perhaps be revisited in some trusts so that a senior financial director or manager reports to the COO instead.

5. It is important that MATs do more to regularly audit the skills, talents and experiences of staff, and how these may contribute

to the work of multi-academy trusts and their schools through 'talent directories'. HR leaders within trusts should seek to identify these additional or complementary skills of both teachers and support staff in order to ensure strategic recruitment, filling gaps in additional skills that may benefit schools across the trust. One example cited included recruiting site managers across schools with complementary skills and experiences – as joiners, electricians and plumbers – so that the trust can better draw upon and deploy 'in house' resources across schools according to need and expertise. This approach is often driven by a good Chief Operating Officer – a role that can readily bring HR and procurement together with finance and new models of service delivery. MATs should also think about how they might use the existing expertise and experience across the MAT to offer a wider range of training and development opportunities, as well as developing more 'in house' services for schools. This audit should extend to administrative staff, premises staff, teaching assistants, and others.

6. Recognise that, as the employer, the trust board has a responsibility to challenge where they consider efficiencies and/or income could be made, as well as to ensure the wellbeing and motivation of all staff within the trust. Many MATs still demonstrate unnecessary duplication of roles across schools – particularly with regard to administrative, technical support and site management roles.

7. When considering whether and how to partner with another MAT or organisation to deliver shared services, always start discussions on the basis of competition – that way you can be open and transparent about the areas where you are in direct competition, and then rapidly move the discussion on to where there may be opportunities for partnership and mutual benefits.

Skills and experience

1. There needs to be a shift in mindset within the MAT sector to adopt a more (ethical) entrepreneurial approach and be willing to be brave and take calculated risks, in particular with regard to income generation through services that also benefit pupils.

2. MATs need to consider how they might collaborate with regard to fundraising opportunities, as well as with regard to bidding for funding. MATs must also be discerning about what they bid for in a climate where it is tempting to pursue multiple opportunities for funding. Some funding streams are not sustainable as – whilst tempting in an era of tighter funding – they may not be aligned with their wider organisational strategy or business plans.

3. MAT trustees can play an important role in generating social capital within their communities to the benefit of trusts and their schools – whilst also being mindful of potential conflicts of interest. Where this happens, it should be recognised and celebrated by trusts and the DfE.

4. Trusts should acknowledge that individual schools within MATs know their communities better than those at the centre – and are, therefore, better placed to consider how best to engage their communities in the activities (including fundraising and opportunities for volunteerism) of both the school and wider MAT. MATs should think carefully about the remit of their local advisory/governing boards in generating local social and professional capital.

5. MATs should consider how developing closer links with the commercial sector can not only increase the skills available to MATs – including via membership on trust boards – but can also open up opportunities to engage with such organisations' CSR (corporate social responsibility) activities, potentially generating a regular additional source of income through sponsored events.

6. All MATs should replicate the successful approach of many HEIs in devising schemes to maintain contact with their school/MAT alumni – again, with potential benefits from both fundraising and social capital perspectives.

7. MAT CEOs should consider appointing a well-qualified COO early on in the MAT's development, and be open to looking beyond the sector and paying a bit more to secure the right individual for the role – they may well be able to make their own salary back (and

more) once established through the efficiencies they achieve and the income they are able to secure. A Chief Finance Officer, whilst in a good position to provide strategic budgeting and achieve better procurement, may not have the experience of developed integrated operations and new models of delivery that give rise to sustainable approaches; such as traded services, fundraising, external relations, and deploying talent more strategically across a MAT to save external contractor costs.

Government support for trusts and ensuring a values-led approach

1. There is a need for the DfE and wider government to emphasise the positive work taking place in many MATs on achieving sustainability – reducing costs and improving services. The government should also be highlighting the excellent practice found within some smaller and medium sized MATs – rather than repeatedly celebrating the same large national MATs.

2. There is a need for the DfE to decide what its school improvement strategy is at a national level, and how MATs and other players fit into this. Too much duplication and complexity in school improvement strategies is leading to more cost and a lack of efficiency in places.

3. The DfE should look at developing a 'seed funding' initiative for MATs to work together to design and develop cross-trust services – including high quality catering, education psychology services, ICT services and others – that address external supplier costs and improve provision for pupils. Services designed by MATs for MATs could result in higher quality provision for pupils, at lower costs than if provided by private profit-making providers, and with better accountability attached to the service. Any funding initiative should look to build these elements in as success criteria.

4. MATs need to be better at telling their stories and sharing the narrative around the work of the sector, including being willing to participate in the development of case studies that can be shared across the sector, as well as with other sectors.

5. MATs need to consider how best to communicate with their communities, as well as with the DfE, about the efficiencies they are achieving, the way in which they are improving services, and the income some of them they generating to the benefit of their schools and pupils. This is important so that they are not seen as commercial 'beasts' but as values-led organisations, with moral purpose around securing the best outcomes for children and young people at their core. Some MATs are doing excellent work in retaining more funding in the sector by providing alternative services to those offered by private providers.

6. As such, MATs need to consider how to analyse, record and share the impact that their activities around sustainability are having on improving educational outcomes and life chances for the children and young people they serve, both within and beyond their MATs and local communities.